LORD,
have you got a minute?

Other books by the author:

Who's in Charge Here?
Stranger in the Pew
The Church Creative (initial chapter)
Pro, Con and Coffee

LORD,
have you got a minute?

Kenneth Wray Conners

Judson Press ® Valley Forge

LORD, HAVE YOU GOT A MINUTE?

Library of Congress Cataloging in Publication Data

Conners, Kenneth Wray.
   Lord, have You got a minute?

   1. Meditations. 2. Christian life—Methodist authors. I. Title.
BV4832.2.C627   248'.48'7   78-15297
ISBN 0-8170-0816-0

Contents

*To that incredible family in Christ:
the ministers, ordained and lay,
of the First United Methodist Church
of Germantown,
with gratitude and affection*

A Symbol of What?

Let not yours be the outward adorning with braiding of hair, decoration of gold, and wearing of fine clothing, but let it be the hidden person of the heart with the imperishable jewel of a gentle and quiet spirit, which in God's sight is very precious (1 Peter 3:3-4).

It is among the most popular
and fashionable
items of jewelry today, Lord,
available in a wide variety of designs,
materials,
sizes, and prices.

Some are severely plain, almost primitive,
and made of wood, leather, plastic, or iron.

Others are quite exotic,
suggestive of the Near East,
and are made in intricate designs expressive of their ethnic
        origin.

Many are costly,
made as they are of silver, gold, platinum,
or other precious metals,
often inlaid with diamonds, rubies, amethysts, or pearls
to accent some decorative motif.

All of which raises a basic
and perhaps disturbing
question:
with so much emphasis on design
and decoration
and chic,
  how many of the wearers
  have given serious thought
  to the sweeping significance
  of a symbol
  as revolutionary as the cross?

In what spirit do they wear the symbol?
Is it simply a piece of decorative jewelry?
Or a token of special privilege,
even of status?
Or is it worn with a full appreciation
that it imposes a heavy obligation
on anyone who reflects
on the meaning of the cross?
Which is to say, that even as Jesus
struggled to bear his cross up to Calvary,
so we, as Christians, should struggle
to defeat the forces of greed,
corruption, and inhumanity
which daily repeat the scandal of the crucifixion
against the poor, the powerless, the forsaken,
the very people Jesus sought to serve.

In a sense, Lord, the variety of crosses we see today
epitomizes the variety of concepts of Christianity
we encounter among those who identify
with Christ and his church.

The ostentatious, decorative, bejeweled cross
reminds us of the ecclesiastics and lay people
who stress religiosity above servanthood,
who are inordinately concerned with liturgy,
with altar appointments, with vestments,
with stained-glass windows,
and with all the other physical appurtenances
which add up to what someone (not Freud)
has called an "edifice complex."

But observe, Lord, that we said *"inordinately* concerned"
with these liturgical and symbolic niceties.
We would not want to imply that the absence of beauty
fosters the worship of God.
We recall that your Son had words of praise
for the woman who broke the alabaster jar of costly ointment
and poured it over his head
as evidence of her love and devotion.
In the same spirit, Lord, we enhance our worship of you
through the beauty of music,
architecture and art,
drama and dance,
and all other forms of aesthetic expression.

But these must not become an end in themselves,
an ostentatious spectacle, an extravaganza
glorifying persons.
Rather, they should lift the human spirit
to a grateful awareness
that you, Lord,
are the author and source
of all beauty, all creativity.

The costly cross of gold, silver, or platinum, Lord,

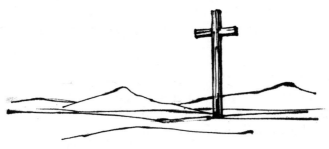

reminds us of churchgoers who equate religion
with prestige, power, privilege, and possessions.
These persons choose their churches
much as they choose their clubs
or their motorcars
or their places of residence.

Do they convey an impression of affluence?
Are they prestigious and exclusive?
Do they reflect good taste?
And do they bring them into contact
with the right people
and the right God?
(not the awe-inspiring God of Moses
but the material god of Mammon;
not the disturbing God of Jeremiah
but the soothing god of positive thinking;
not the loving, self-sacrificing God of Jesus
but the self-indulgent god of hedonism.)

Their concern about associating with the "right people"
inevitably brings them face-to-face
with the annoying question raised by James
in his letter to the twelve tribes
in the Dispersion:

"For if a man with gold rings and in fine clothing
comes into your assembly,
and a poor man in shabby clothing
also comes in,
and you pay attention to the one who wears the fine
clothing
and say,
'Have a seat here, please,'
while you say to the poor man,
'Stand there,' or, 'sit at my feet,'
have you not made distinctions among yourselves,
and become judges with evil thoughts?"

To which they are likely to respond:
"Lord, don't confront us with problems such as these;
instead, help us keep the church exclusive
and we shall not even have to see the poor man!"

Above all else, they ask, is the church successful,
which is to say, is its membership growing?
Is its financial position secure?
And does it support, and refuse to question,
the values of our economic system
despite its many inequities,
the nature of our social order
with all its injustices,
and the integrity of our nation's policies?

Affirmative answers to questions such as these
should assure each churchgoer complete religious freedom
from embarrassment,
from anxiety,
from involvement in any possible challenge
to the sacred status quo!

And lastly, Lord, the plain cross of wood, leather, or iron
by the simplicity of its design
and the strength and character of its materials
reminds us of those ministers and laypersons
who strive to keep the spirit of Christ
at the center of their daily living.
They see in the cross a poignant reminder
of evil's fleeting triumph
over your Son,
but the absence of his crucified body
from the cross
also reminds them of his ultimate victory
over death.
They also see in the cross a sobering symbol
of the way in which life's vertical dimension,
your spiritual power, love, and compassion,
meets and intersects the horizontal dimension,
our daily relations with our neighbors
on planet Earth.

All of which, Lord, makes of the cross a challenge
to everyone bold enough to claim the title
"Christian."

And what is the challenge?

> Simply to acknowledge that if Christ,
> the suffering servant,
> is to befriend and help his struggling humanity,
> it is our privilege and our mission, as Christians,
> to participate personally in the incarnation.

O Lord, can there be any blessing
> more to be desired
> than to enable someone to catch a glimpse
> of the living Christ
> in us?

Amen.

*The Scripture quoted in the text of the prayer
is from James 1:2-4.*

Anatomy of Loneliness

If I ascend up into heaven, thou art there; if I make my bed in hell, behold, thou art there! If I take the wings of the morning, and dwell in the uttermost parts of the sea; Even there shall thy hand lead me, and thy right hand shall hold me (Psalm 139:8-10, KJV).

Why is it, Lord, that we constantly assail our ears
with strident sounds made by humans?

Whether in restaurant, supermarket, or shop,
in waiting room, lounge, or bar,
in elevator or jet plane awaiting takeoff,
we find ourselves surrounded by music.

> Down sidewalks teenage troubadours stroll,
> their radios raucous with rock,
> while storefront speakers add to the din
> in deafening decibels.

> Along broad highways, cars with CBs
> echo electronic chatter,
> while in thousands of homes, TVs and stereos
> inhibit conversation.

If silence is indeed golden, Lord,
why have we gone off the gold standard?
Does the absence of sound
strike fear in our hearts
because it intensifies
our feelings of loneliness?

> And are we afraid of being alone
> amidst the city's millions
> because we feel so remote, so alienated
> from our brothers and sisters?

Or is it that we are haunted, Lord,
by an even greater fear,
fear that we are alienated from you
whose death some theologians
once tried to proclaim,
while others hail this very urban anonymity
as a boon to us and not a source of frustration and despair
which drives us up a wall?

Little wonder, Lord, that those in prison
fear the threat of solitary,
regarding it as the most cruel sentence,
the ultimate in penal loneliness.

But if there are degrees of loneliness,
the one we find most awesome to our souls
disturbs us each time we contemplate
the vastness of your starry universe;
when we are forced to measure in the millions
the years light takes to come from distant stars,
our lonely selves appear like grains of sand
upon the beach of your eternity.

> That, Lord, is a loneliness so profound
> it raises crucial questions:
> Who am I?
> Who are you?
> Where are we headed?
> For what purpose?
> And when do we meet you
> face to face?

Until such time as interstellar space
reveals its secrets
and perhaps diminishes the mystery,
doesn't it behoove us, Lord,
to go about your work
and follow the example of your Son
by relating creatively
to those about us close at hand?

Look at their faces
as we walk down a busy city street!
See their withdrawn expressions,
eyes which avert as they meet ours,
lips tense, chins resolute,
and scarcely a smile
in a block of plodding humanity.

How many are secretly yearning
for some nod of recognition,
some casual word of greeting,
some acknowledgment that they, too, are human?

Yet, Lord, how often we sentence them
and ourselves
to solitary confinement
by hiding our inner feelings behind a façade
of sophistication,
or self-sufficiency,
or smug superiority
(or is it simply shyness that restrains us?)

And how rewarding can be the effort,
seldom rebuffed,
to break through the barriers
and establish contact with a stranger!
The friendly nod that transforms a dour countenance
into an answering smile;
the pleasantry that draws an appreciative chuckle
and brightens an otherwise dreary day;
the casual conversation that discloses a mutual interest
and launches an enriching acquaintance.

And as we begin to diminish our loneliness, Lord,
by discovering how many others share our aspirations,

hopes, and fears,
we find our anxiety diminishing
about you and your ultimate purpose for us.
We begin to realize that we need each other,
that we are not alone,
that we can help establish a sense of community
wherever we are.

> Oh, yes, your universe still is vast,
> your mystery impenetrable,
> your nature beyond our comprehension.
> But we begin to embrace the truth of the psalmist:
> "If I ascend up into heaven,
> thou art there;
> if I make my bed in hell,
> behold, thou art there.
> If I take the wings of the morning,
> and dwell in the uttermost parts of the sea;
> Even there shall thy hand lead me,
> and thy right hand shall hold me."

So our loneliness can be transmuted into solitude
which is to be valued, not feared,
for the opportunity it provides us
> to reflect,
> to marvel,
> to be grateful
for this magnificent world you have given us
peopled by so many amazing human beings,
and to ponder your goodness,
> your love,
> your concern and compassion
as we have seen it embodied
in your Son, Jesus.

> Thank you, Lord, for solitude
> and for helping us to help others
> overcome loneliness.

Amen.

Lost Horizons

I said to myself "Come now, I will make a test of pleasure; enjoy yourself." But behold, this also was vanity. I said of laughter, "It is mad," and of pleasure, "What use is it?" (Ecclesiastes 2:1-2).

Her brow was furrowed, Lord,
and her eyes glistened strangely
in the early morning sunlight
as if she were struggling to hold back tears.
"I'm forty, now, you know," she confided,
like one revealing the age of the Pyramids,
"and I simply must find happiness.
So I've decided to return to the West Coast
where there are many resources
to help persons like me."

And then, after a pause,
and with an almost pathetic wistfulness, she asked,
"Is it wrong to seek happiness?"

Mark well that question, Lord,
for if it *is* wrong,
a multitude of your children
are caught up in a sin of monstrous proportions.
For we live in a society
that exalts the pursuit of happiness
and offers rich rewards to the entertainer,
the athlete, and the provider of gourmet food.

But observe, Lord, how often the pursuit
becomes a frantic personal quest
for self-fulfillment,
for self-gratification,
sometimes to a point of
self-destruction!

    Are you unhappy?
    Then try Gestalt group therapy.
    Are you frustrated?
    Get in touch with your basic impulses
    via the primal scream.
    Are you unable to relate?
    Perhaps Transactional Analysis will help.

Do you feel cut off from your roots?
You may need the experience of rebirthing.
Are your body rhythms irregular?
Why not investigate biokinetics?
Is your mate unresponsive?
Try a Marriage Encounter marathon.
Do you have difficulty pulling it all together?
Get yourself a mantra
and Transcendental Meditation may help.
Are you in conflict with your innermost urges?
Let EST demolish your ego, drive you up a wall,
then restructure your personality.
Is your approach to life negative, apprehensive?
Then concentrate on "I'm okay . . . you're okay."
Do feelings of inadequacy assail you?
Jungian dream analysis may reveal
your subconscious hang-ups.

And so, Lord, whether our seeker after happiness
embraces one of these panaceas
or, instead, turns to a guru
or to some form of zen or yoga,
or embarks on a drug-induced trip,
basically her problem reflects insecurity
aggravated by an intense preoccupation with self.
Although she may discern on some horizon
the place where heaven and earth seem to meet,
the farther toward her distant goal she trudges
the farther it recedes beyond her reach.

In this narcissistic age when souls
are preyed upon by those in search of gain,
    assailed by advertisers,
    manipulated by the media,
    pressured by peers,
    browbeaten by bosses,
    patronized by politicians,
    cajoled to become conspicuous consumers,
what is your prescription, Lord,
for finding a full and satisfying life?

But wait! You've already given us
the answer in the person of your Son,
this man for others who, with selfless zeal,
daily ministered to those in need.
In charging us to love and serve our neighbor
by feeding the hungry,
giving drink to the thirsty,
welcoming the stranger,
clothing the naked,
visiting the sick and the prisoner,
He's shown us how to live a useful life
without recourse to psychiatric props.

For happiness, dear Lord, is not an end
but, instead, a gift we may receive,
a rich by-product of our basic task
of doing well the work you ask of us.
Our pilgrimage from the cradle to the grave
offers joy if we can learn to grow
from ego-worship to concern for others,
from self-indulgence to self-sacrifice,
from love of self to love of God and neighbor,
and then, most difficult of all to master,
the art of loving enemy like friend.

So, Lord, we find ourselves confronted daily
with a crucial question each must face:
if we choose to lavish on ourselves
almost all the love we have to share,
how much love remains
to bestow on others?

Amen.

Sixty-five

I hated all my toil in which I had toiled under the sun, seeing that I must leave it to the man who will come after me; and who knows whether he will be a wise man or a fool? Yet he will be master of all for which I toiled and used my wisdom under the sun. This also is vanity (Ecclesiastes 2:18-29).

"Therefore do not be anxious about tomorrow, for tomorrow will be anxious for itself. Let the day's own trouble be sufficient for the day" (Matthew 6:34).

There he is, Lord, standing beside the podium,
a slight figure but with a noticeable paunch,
his receding hair now gray, streaked with white,
a wan smile on his face
as the president and chief executive officer of the firm
presents him with the traditional gold watch
to the applause of the hundred diners in the banquet room,
faces flushed after too many visits to the cash bar.

He has listened, a bit ruefully,
to the three preceding speakers
as they recounted
in extravagant words and lilting cadences
the significant contributions he has made

to the success of the corporation
during the past forty years.

He thought the accolades sounded overstated, inflated,
like a eulogy for the deceased at a funeral service
and not in keeping,
he reflected with a touch of bitterness,
with the size of the modest salary increases
he had been receiving down through the years.

But enough of bittersweet, nostalgic reminiscences!
This was to be a triumphal event, a joyous climax,
something of a corporate graduation.

A graduation from what?

Well, Lord, a graduation
from the ranks of the gainfully employed,
leaving behind him the private office
with his name lettered on the door,
the telephones, the intercom, the secretary,
the electronic beeper
tucked in his breast pocket,
the seat in the executive dining room
and all the other symbols
of corporate status;

a graduation
from a triballike business community
with its defined hierarchy of chiefs,
assistants to the chief,
assistant chiefs
down to the rank-and-file Indians
including, he recalled
with a sardonic chuckle,
the tribal medicine man
known and feared by the title
"Psychological Consultant,"
a man skilled at shrinking skulls
to whatever dimension
the personnel evaluation committee
considered expedient;

a graduation from the security of the corporate reservation
   with its proscribed time
   for each part of the daily ritual:
   "Good morning, Miss Jones; Morning, Rogers;
   Morning, Cahill; Good morning, Miss Spencer";
   the in-basket full; the out-basket empty;
   staff meeting at ten, and don't forget the coffee;
   hold all phone calls until further notice;
   it must be Friday, for Payroll's Betty Clark
   is making the rounds with the weekly wampum;
   12:15 and time for lunch,
   which signals the scramble to beat old Thomas
   to a seat at the president's table;
   it's P.M. and pell-mell to finish out the week's work;
   "No time, Miss Spencer, to see Charlie Scott";
   deadline at four for the revised budget figures;
   sign out letters; return those phone calls;
   the in-basket empty; the out-basket full;
   time to break and run for the 5:14!

Yes, Lord, it is a graduation from business busyness,
from the daily round of contacts
with colleagues, chiefs, competitors,
from the mad struggle for results, recognition, rewards,
from a personhood shaped by loyalty
to the corporate ethos.

   And if it resembles a graduation
   how like a commencement it is, too!

   But a commencement, Lord, of what?

The answer becomes a source
of frustration, fear, and phobias, on the one hand,
or a basis for expectation, enthusiasm, and enterprise,
depending upon the thoughts which race through his mind.

"Commencement! Are you kidding?
I'm not one of those college seniors with most of their lives
before them!
At sixty-five, the major part of my life is over.
How many years—or how few—lie ahead?"

"And which of you by being anxious
can prolong his life a single moment?"

"And supposing I do live to an old age,
until eighty or eighty-five or ninety?
How will I manage it financially?
Will my pension, Social Security, and other income
enable me to survive the inflation ahead?"

"Therefore do not be anxious about tomorrow,
for tomorrow will be anxious for itself."

"And why, at sixty-five, toss me on the trash heap?
Is all this talk of conservation and ecology
simply talk?
Doesn't it apply to humans?
If beer cans can be recycled,
why, in God's name, can't I?"

"Look at the birds of the air:
they neither sow nor reap nor gather into barns,
and yet your heavenly Father feeds them.
Are you not of more value than they?"

"And, Lord, I feel so alone!
My decisions at the corporation
involved much consultation with colleagues—
advice, cross-checks, and approvals!
Now I feel isolated,
like a lone skipper on a dark sea,
sailing a ship without compass, crew, or constellations
to guide him
yet facing difficult choices as to direction,
the geographic environment most congenial,
the mode of life most suitable,
even how freely, or cautiously, we may indulge
in life's little pleasures!"

" Therefore do not be anxious, saying:
'What shall we eat?' or 'What shall we drink?'
or 'What shall we wear?'
But seek first his kingdom and his righteousness,
and all these things shall be yours as well."

"Is my future to be an aimless, monotonous round
of golf, bridge, and happy hours?
Is that all there is in store for me, Lord,
just marking time until the inevitable health crisis
suddenly assails my mind or body?"

> " And he who had received the five talents came forward,
> bringing five talents more, saying:
> 'Master, you delivered to me five talents;
> here I have made five talents more.'
> His master said to him,
> 'Well done, good and faithful servant;
> you have been faithful over a little,
> I will set you over much;
> enter into the joy of your master.'"

Thank you, Lord, for offering us alternatives
to the aging/anxiety/panic syndrome
which often afflicts otherwise stable senior citizens.

All is *not* over at sixty-five!

We reflect on the accomplishments
of such imaginative, talented oldsters
as Pablo Casals, Leopold Stokowski, Igor Stravinsky,
Dr. Paul Dudley White, Albert Schweitzer, Sigmund Freud,
King Gustav VI of Sweden, Norman Thomas,
Sir Winston Churchill,

Frank Lloyd Wright, Pablo Picasso, Grandma Moses,
Agatha Christie, Pearl Buck, George Bernard Shaw,
Harry Emerson Fosdick, Karl Barth, Roland Bainton,
to name just a few
from the present and recent past,
    and we marvel!

Opportunity beckons to each of us, too,
whether we are one-talent, two-talent,
or five-talent persons
with five, ten, or twenty-five years ahead of us.
Little wonder that more and more persons today
are approaching retirement
with eagerness, enthusiasm, and expectation,
recognizing that this can be life's most deeply satisfying stage
for which they have long been in rehearsal.

It is only necessary that we hear and heed Christ's call,
"Follow me,"
and open ourselves to the world and its humanity.

For there are people to be befriended and served,
youth to be encouraged and guided,
causes to be championed and fought for,
music to be composed,
poems to be penned,
art to be created,
discoveries to be made
whether we are forty, sixty, or eighty!

But are you, Mr. and Mrs. Retiree, still skeptical?
Still uneasy about the future?
Still reluctant to venture forth
with confidence and with faith?

Then consider how you would react
if you faced this hypothetical situation:

Imagine for a moment that you are retiring,
not at sixty-five,
but at the midpoint of your career
while you are only thirty.
And imagine that you have remaining
not ten, twenty, or thirty years
but only three!

What then?

How would you view the future?
Would you push forward energetically?
Or would you "give up" and protest that three years
is not time enough
to accomplish anything worthwhile?

Yet this was not a hypothetical,
but an actual historic situation,
two thousand years ago!

We remember, Lord, that Jesus of Nazareth
earned his livelihood as a carpenter
while preparing for his future calling.
Earlier he had given intimations of greatness when
as a youth
he had asked such precocious questions
of the learned teachers at the temple
that they were amazed at his insights and comprehension.
And then, after having been known for thirty years
simply as Joseph's son,
he retired from his occupation to mount a ministry
so miraculous
that it transformed the world
in the short span of three years,
    bringing new hope, new visions, new life
    to people everywhere—
        even to us.

                    Amen.

The Scriptures quoted in the text of this prayer
are found in Matthew 6:27, The Twentieth Century
New Testament, *and Matthew 6:34, 26, 31, 33.*

The Time of Our Lives

For everything there is a season,
and a time for every matter under heaven:
>   a time to be born, and a time to die; . . .
>   a time to weep, and a time to laugh; . . .
>   a time to seek, and a time to lose;
>   a time to keep, and a time to cast away;
>   a time to rend, and a time to sew;
>   a time to keep silence, and a time to speak;
>   a time to love, and a time to hate;
>   a time for war, and a time for peace.
>   (Ecclesiastes 3:1, 2, 4, 6, 7, 8)

Every fifteen minutes came the sound of the Westminster
        chimes,
clear and with metallic brilliance upon the still night air
pealing from the lofty belltower
of the massive Durham cathedral
just up the hill from our university dormitory rooms
in northeastern England.

Then, following every fourth quarter-hour,
after an expectant pause

as if a hushed audience were awaiting an encore,
came the heavy, ponderous bass requiem.

There was something almost grim,
　　　authoritative,
　　　relentless
in the tolling of the hour,
each measured stroke of the hammer
bearing down with monotonous, insistent finality
as though some invisible deity
were emphasizing the fragility of life,
the fleeting perishability of time,
and the departure of yet another hour
　　　never to return.

On this overnight stop with my wife
I had intended to continue my writing
no later than midnight,
but something about those tower chimes
seemed to break in upon my consciousness
at shorter and shorter intervals throughout the evening
as though some evil little person
were speeding up the clock mechanism
making me uneasily aware, Lord,
of how swiftly time can pass.

And so, when the twelfth stroke of midnight boomed forth,
I continued to clutch pen and pad compulsively
groping for the right word, ever elusive,
with a new sense of urgency and haste.

　　　Will there be time enough
　　　to finish the task at hand?
　　　To accomplish all of those ambitious plans
　　　which the human mind can conceive
　　　and the mind of God can cut short?
　　　Will time fly by at an even faster rate
　　　as the months and years pass?
　　　Will a misguided sense of urgency
　　　sacrifice hard-earned pleasures
　　　on the guilt-stained altar of duty?

Questions such as these
seldom assail the young
who fancy their lives stretching before them
into the never-ending distance.

How providential, Lord, that in your scheme of things
childhood is a time for leisurely exploration,
a time for discovering the novelty of persons and places,
a time for wondering and wandering,
  for testing and trusting,
  for hurting and healing,
  for playing and pretending,
  for loving and laughing,
  for germinating and growing.

All this can make of childhood
a blessed preparation for the future
  or a trauma of warped views and emotions.
The difference, Lord, is in your presence
  or absence.

How providential, Lord, that in your scheme of things
youth is a time for adjusting to life's demands,
a time for making mistakes
while there's still time to mend
and make amends,
a time for wasting time before it's rationed,
a time for cutting cords and tying knots,
a time for dreams and doubts,
  for fads and fancies,
  for heroes and heroines,
  for romance and rebellion,
  for marriage and mating,
  for children and careers.
All this can make of youth
a maturing time for discovering our true identity
  or a frantic time for donning a disguise.
The difference, Lord, is in your presence
  or absence.

How providential, Lord, that in your scheme of things
adulthood is a time for accomplishment,
a time for striving to adjust life to us
while asking how much, or how little, is enough,
a time for putting first things first or last,
a time for selfless serving or self-seeking,
    for altruism or acquisitiveness,
    for virtue or villainy,
    for integrity or infidelity,
    for uprightness or uptightness,
    for tenderness or toughness,
    for finding you or forsaking you.
All this can make of adulthood
a time for shouldering personal and social responsibilities
    or a time for cold-shouldering human need.
The difference, Lord, is your presence
    or absence.

How providential, Lord, that in your scheme of things
mid-life is a time of reassessment,
a time for recognizing that we are mortal
as from afar we sense the chill of death,
a time for looking critically at marriage
and adolescently at sexy options,
a time for reappraising one's career
in the light of dreams now unfulfilled,
a time for coping or for copping out,
    for philosophizing or psychiatrizing,
    for faithfulness or faithlessness,
    for humility or haughtiness,
    for harmony or hostility,
    for devotion or disaffection
    for self-denial or self-love,
    for new perspectives or old prejudices.
All this can make of mid-life
a time for pulling it all together
    or apart!
The difference, Lord, is your presence
    or absence.

How providential, Lord, that in your scheme of things
the later years can be a time of fulfillment
and self-realization,
a time when childhood traits are now amplified
for better or for worse!
a time when conservation of energy becomes a reality
as knowledge and experience lead to shortcuts
and less wasted time,
a time when creativity can function at a high level
and not be squandered on impressing others,
a time for deepening of friendships,
        for the shedding of excess baggage,
        for self-discipline or self-indulgence,
        for frugality or free-spending,
        for self-confidence or shyness,
        for sociability or seclusion,
        for congeniality or coolness,
        for thankfulness or thanklessness,
        for readjustment to new times or rigid clinging to old,
        for saintliness or sanctimoniousness.
All this can make of the later years
a time for a paradiselike existence
        or purgatory!
The difference, Lord, is your presence
        or absence.

As we look back over our lives, Lord,
or look ahead to the future,
how wonderful to contemplate that Christ really is
"the man for all seasons"!

He is timeless; yet
he identifies with us, and we with him,
        in childhood,
        in youth,
        in adulthood,
        in mid-life,
        in our later years.

It is his presence
and our sensitivity to that presence
which really makes this
"the time of our lives."

Have you ever met persons who yearn for eternity
yet who don't know what to do with a rainy Sunday afternoon?
Preserve us, dear Lord, from falling into the easy trap
of focusing our eyes on the life eternal
and failing to see what you would have us do
for our brothers and sisters on planet Earth.

Yes, heaven and hell are not merely concepts
reserved for some future existence
but part and parcel of conditions around us
as we experience the time of our lives.

> Whether we contribute to the one or the other
> is in our hands . . . linked with yours!

> Amen.

One-Way Ticket

"And which of you by being anxious can prolong his life a single moment?"
(Matthew 6:27, *The Twentieth Century New Testament*)

It happened again last week, Lord!
Suddenly the word began to be whispered,
passing from person to person
through taut, tensed lips
like some sibilant hiss
of a deadly viper
inducing not only fear in each listener
but also a morbid sense of fascination.

> "Have you heard the terrible news
> about Marjorie?"
> Then, after an uneasy pause,
> "She has cancer."

For each hearer, the shock was unsettling,
the distress, deeply felt,
the frustration, akin to anger;

anger often directed at you, Lord,
for permitting this cruel misfortune
to assail a woman so young,
with children so small and helpless,
and with so much of life
still to be savored and enjoyed.

But then, Lord, began a ministry
of love and compassion
that was beautiful to behold.
To her hospital room came so many loyal friends
they had to be scheduled in relays;
flowers in profusion filled every nook and cranny
while from persons who had only casually known her
came a veritable deluge of cards and notes
expressing concern, compassion, and cheer.
Relationships, formerly friendly but casual,
became tender, loving, and supportive,
as young and old alike
glimpsed Marjorie's inner beauty
and admired her courage.

In the meantime, back at her home,
neighbors almost seemed to be vying with one another
to provide meals and perform household chores
for Marjorie's worried husband
and their three perplexed children.

And what of Marjorie's morale during this trying time?
Lord, she was an inspiration to us all,
as those who came to offer comfort
found themselves, instead, being comforted.

> Her first plaintive cry, "Why me, Lord?"
> gave way to a philosophic, "Why *not* me?"
> as it was borne in on her
> in a poignantly personal way
> that we all are mortal,
> vulnerable to the vicissitudes
> of this beautiful but hazardous universe
> you created.

Why is it, Lord, that until we encounter problems,
so often the best in us lies dormant?
Strengths we didn't know exist now surface;
we receive the grace to empathize,
whereas success can make us cool and callous,
indifferent to the needs of those around us
as though another's trouble was your way
of showing your displeasure with that life,
freeing us from any obligation
to love each brother, sister, as ourselves.

> And since not one of us can foretell
> the time or place of his or her demise,
> why, O Lord, do we so often wait
> until misfortune strikes
> before we pause to thank you
> for the priceless worth of those around us
> and then make certain that they hear from us
> words expressing all they mean to us?

So help us, Lord, to live each day
as though another might not dawn,
savoring to the fullest
the unique personhood of all we meet
by granting them ample time and space
to show us who they really are
and what they seek.

Grant us, too, Lord, the sensitivity
to comprehend the words they speak
(and those unspoken yearnings of the heart)
that we may respond to their needs
not merely physically
but also at deeper emotional and psychological levels,
for we will not come this way again.

Lord, you have given us a one-way ticket
to an unknown destination
on a journey shrouded in mystery,
but as long as we are aware
that you are conducting our pilgrimage,
we shall travel onward with faith
and confidence.

Amen.

Politician
or Prophetic
Preacher?

Am I now seeking the favor of men, or of God? Or am I trying to please men? If
I were still pleasing men, I should not be a servant of Christ (Galatians 1:10).

They have become highly successful churches, Lord,
by promulgating a gospel of positive thinking,
by emphasizing that with you
all material blessings are possible,
by promising personal salvation, happiness,
and the life abundant,
and by worshiping the sanctity of the status quo.
    Father, forgive!

Each year, their membership rolls and attendances grow,
their budgets increase impressively,
their income from pledges climbs,
as statistically they attest to the popularity
of theological tranquilizers.
    Father, have mercy!

Their pastors are highly paid,
    highly praised,
    highly privileged,
always in demand to make a foursome at the club,
admired for their sympathetic understanding
of the problems of the well-to-do,
sought after to speak at Rotary, Kiwanis, and other meetings.
    Father, enlighten!

By contrast, there are certain other churches, Lord,
where the pastors earnestly strive to show their people
how contrary to the teachings of Jesus
is this affluent living of ours
while in distant lands hundreds of millions starve.
Preaching prophetically, these pastors point to history
and to you,
suggesting corrective measures we should adopt
if this widespread misery and suffering are to be ameliorated.
    Father, bless!

But the statistics of these churches, Lord,
    are not encouraging.
Frequently there is little or no growth in membership.
Meeting the budget brings on a yearly crisis.
The pastor risks accusations of leftist leanings
from community leaders who view his opinions
as unjustified attacks on the American way of life.
    Father, sustain!

What we are seeing, Lord, are two pastoral philosophies:
one based on telling the pew-sitter
what he or she wants to hear
in an urbane, entertaining manner
so that the pastor, like a politician,
keeps in favor with his "electorate"
in order to maintain a firm grip on the pulpit position;
   the other based on challenging the pew-sitter
   continually to rethink
   his or her priorities and value judgments
   in the light of the apostle Paul's admonition
   not to conform to the world's standards
   but to be transformed by the renewal of our minds.

Now all this raises a fundamental question about the laity:
if the pastor preaches what the layperson wants to hear
or even what the layperson is *willing* to hear
without rebellion, recrimination, or retaliation,
what limitations does this place on the clergy?
What is the laity's basic understanding
of the Christian gospel
and its relevancy for our time?
The answer is crucially important, Lord,
for, in practice, the laity *is* the church;
their attitudes, prejudices, and expectations
largely determine its nature, vitality,
effectiveness, and mission,
more so, in fact, than all the weighty pronouncements
of bishops, moderators, council presidents,
and others of the ecclesiastical hierarchy.
　　Is the gospel to be a living reality,
　　with revolutionary impact upon our lives
　　and upon society?
　　Or is it to be a static, unchanging body of tradition
　　with constraints on innovation and spiritual growth?

Looked at in another light—
the laity goes to the theater and pays to be entertained;
is it willing to attend church and pay
to be challenged, confronted, disturbed, and renewed?

If these considerations pose a dilemma
for conscientious clergypersons today
who want to lead their people in a prophetic way
into a fuller understanding of the mind of Christ,
　　yet not be attacked, harassed, even ostracized
　　by forces of reaction inside and outside the church,
think of the tensions which the apostle Paul must have felt
as this missionary-pastor-founder of infant churches
struggled to proclaim the Good News
amidst the hostility of the Judaizers,
the persecution of the pagans,
and the antagonism of the Roman authorities who were
ever alert to any threat to their power.

Little wonder that Paul had to proceed cautiously
in applying this new gospel to social issues!
With hundreds of thousands of slaves in Rome
and serfdom an integral part of the economic system,
he dared not, for example, preach the abolition of slavery.
Instead, he urged slaves to be obedient to their masters
but at the same time stressed that, in your eyes, Lord,
  "there is neither Jew nor Greek,
  there is neither slave nor free,
  there is neither male nor female;
  for you are all one in Christ Jesus,"
a spiritually comforting affirmation of our basic worth
in your sight
regardless of our status—or lack of it—
in the social order in which we find ourselves.

But unlike Paul, pastors today are not exposed
to such life-threatening extremes of persecution.
Seldom do they risk legal action or incarceration
(although a Berrigan can be jailed
for dramatizing his opposition
to an unjust and undeclared war).
Also, our churches today are well established,
accepted as an essential part of our social fabric,
respectable though not always respected,
prestigious though often lacking in power.
And today, many of the tenets of Christianity—
for example, religious and social freedom for all peoples
regardless of race, belief, sex, economic status,
or national origin—
are recognized in principle by our civil authorities.

  Then why, many argue, should our clergy
  criticize the established social order?
  Better that they confine their activities
  to spiritual matters within their purview!

"I am delighted with all this disillusionment... It's a great time to be religious."

But if pastors fail to speak prophetic words, Lord,
who will confront our secular society
with the compassionate concerns of Christ
for human beings and their well-being?

Will business or industry come to grips
    with Christian priorities vis-à-vis the profit drive?
    Enlightened business leaders may argue for change,
    certain trade associations may set up ethical standards,
    but who but the church can take the broad view
    and provide Christian reference points
    free of self-interest?

And will labor criticize labor's misuse of power?
    Although renegades within unions may fight for reform
    and risk ending their days encased in concrete,
    it is the clergy who can mediate labor disputes
    by bringing Christ's spirit to the negotiating table.

And where, Lord, does the conscience of government reside?
    Not in city hall. Not in state capitols.
    Not in our self-serving federal bureaucracy!
    If the trauma of Watergate taught us anything,
    it is the futility of expecting political leaders
    to forgo special privilege and personal gain
    as long as they are oblivious to Christian concepts
    of public morality.

All this is a challenge, Lord, not only to the clergy
but to the laity as well.
For it is the duty of laypersons
to become partners with their pastors,
to encourage them in their prophetic ministry,
to defend their right to apply the gospel to social problems
and thus maintain a free and courageous pulpit,
to promote dialogue between clergy and laity
in a spirit of mutual respect and understanding,
to help educate those in the congregation
who may feel intimidated by the prospect
of Christ's word really becoming flesh
and dwelling in our economic/social wilderness.

And the laity's role doesn't end here!
For who is to implement the prophetic word
once it is proclaimed?
        Who is to prepare the petitions?
        Participate in the campaigns for justice?
        Call on senators and representatives?
        See that voters turn out for elections?
        Serve on city councils and school boards?
        Work for prison reform
        and the elimination of police brutality?
        Speak up in business and labor meetings
        so that your presence, God, may be felt?

Yes, and who is to be the ethical conscience
of the church and its own affairs?
        Who is to insist that its staff be compensated
        with the same fairness it advocates for industry?
        Who is to make certain that a church's investments
        not only avoid sanctioning corporate malpractice
        but also, more positively, help finance ventures
        which strive to serve socially responsible ends?

A key to this joint clergy-laity partnership
is the spirit in which our culture's flaws and faults
are exposed to Christ's incandescent light.
If it is done with arrogance and self-righteousness
and an insistence that we are the sole custodians of truth,
we are guilty of insufferable religious snobbery
and can only antagonize those we seek to influence.

But if we deal with facts honestly and accurately,
avoid oversimplifying complex issues,
present our convictions calmly, clearly, patiently,
and recognize with compassion the problems faced
by those asked to alter long-standing practices,
we may find that genuinely prophetic voices
are *not* without honor in their own countries.

> The unacceptable alternative is to concede
> that the gospel can change the hearts of persons
> but not their collective actions,
> thus absolving ourselves, clergy and laity alike,
> of responsibility for emulating all those
> who down through history have called into question
> society's inhumanity
> and its disobedience to you, Lord,
> prophets such as Amos, Isaiah, Jeremiah, Ezekiel,
> the apostle Paul and his activism,
> yes, and even Jesus the Christ.

Amen.

*The Scripture quoted in the text of this prayer
is found in Galatians 3:28.*

How Much, and at What Cost?

I made great works; I built houses and planted vineyards for myself; I made myself gardens and parks, and planted in them all kinds of fruit trees. I made myself pools from which to water the forest of growing trees. I bought male and female slaves, and had slaves who were born in my house; I had also great possessions of herds and flocks, more than any who had been before me in Jerusalem. I also gathered for myself silver and gold and the treasure of kings and provinces; I got singers, both men and women, and many concubines, man's delight.

So I became great and surpassed all who were before me in Jerusalem; also my wisdom remained with me. And whatever my eyes desired I did not keep from them; I kept my heart from no pleasure, for my heart found pleasure in all my toil, and this was my reward for all my toil. Then I considered all that my hands had done and the toil I had spent in doing it, and behold, all was vanity and a striving after wind, and there was nothing to be gained under the sun (Ecclesiastes 2:4-11).

How familiar, how modern, how up-to-date
is the man so graphically described
by the writer of Ecclesiastes!

Although his business activities
were not those of today's industrial giants

but, instead, were appropriate
to the agronomist/mercantile economy of his time,
this man clearly was an executive type,
an entrepreneur,
a dynamic builder of empires,
one with power and possessions and pride
    (note especially his pride . . .
    "so I became great
    and surpassed all who were before me
    in Jerusalem"),
a Howard Hughes of his time,
a workaholic!

But although this man derived great satisfaction
from the acquiring of all these possessions—
property, slaves, concubines, silver and gold—
his pleasure was confined
to the act of building, buying,
bartering, grasping, accumulating.
Once acquired,
the sought-after possessions lost their allure
and, after amassing so much wealth,
what next?

Significantly, this man of wealth
several thousand years ago
seems to be lamenting the emptiness of his life
amidst affluence,
much as today's prosperous persons of influence—
despite our vaunted technology, abundance,
and rising gross national product—
so often are heard expressing frantic feelings
of frustration, foreboding, and futility.

    All of which raises a question, Lord:
    are we the possessors of all these material things
    or are we possessed, enslaved and
    dominated by our possessions?
    And if the frenetic pursuit of power and prestige
    is the grim source of many persons' pleasure,
    does that account
    for the workaholic's morbid fear of retirement?

49

Yet technology, Lord, is not *per se* an evil thing!
It is easy to oversimplify and indict all progress
or nostalgically romanticize the joys of the simple life
without acknowledging that science and invention
have virtually eliminated child labor,
the twelve-hour workday,
and punishing, backbreaking toil
by both persons and beasts.
Even the most cynical and critical of our youth
who rant and rail against the tyranny of "the system,"
regard with religious fervor their electronic guitars,
long-playing records,
and stereos!

> But in 1973, Lord, came a significant event
> to shake up our smugness and complacency.
> Our Moslem friends from the East,
> who long had brought us gifts
> of oil, incense, and myrrh,
> suddenly decided
> they no longer would blindly worship
> our god of light, power, and *sic transit gloria.*

With this came a growing realization, Lord,
that we have been raping your beautiful earth,
polluting your lovely limpid lakes and streams,
contaminating your pure air,
even sentencing many industrial workers
to slow, lingering deaths
through the harmful substances given off—
silently, stealthily, secretly—
by certain chemical-processing operations.

Add to this
> a diminution of the world's natural resources,
> unemployment in the midst of prosperity,
> widespread boredom from dull, repetitive tasks
> which rob work of meaning,
> suffering from the maldistribution of wealth.
and even the least sensitive among us
are beginning to realize
that our ecologic-economic-societal binge
is nearing an end,

and a radical change in life-styles
is imperative.

Then we hear our Buddhist friends
expound their threefold doctrine for the good life
which offers a chance for persons
>   to utilize and develop their faculties,
>   to overcome their ego-centeredness by joining with
>   others in a common task,
>   and to produce the goods and services
>   needed for humane existence.

All of which implies pride and self-fulfillment
through the application
of creative skills and craftsmanship,
cooperation with others
instead of mindless competition,
enough of leisure to enjoy the fruits of one's work
and to grow in understanding,
character, and spiritual maturity.

What is to be *our* answer, Lord?
Isn't it incumbent on us to redefine our value system?
To substitute quality of life for quantity of things?
To relearn the disciplines of frugality?
To place the common good ahead of selfish desire?
To realize that "bigger and bigger" can be vulgar
while small *can* be beautiful?

>   But most intriguing of all, Lord, is the thought
>   that our Moslem brothers,
>   by forcing upon us a new awareness of scarcity,
>   and our Buddhist brothers,
>   by placing before us a concept of work
>   designed to enhance, not debase, human dignity,
>   ultimately may help us Christians
>   become more Christian!
>
>   Thanks be to God.

Amen.

Interruptions

"What I tell you in the dark, utter in the light; and what you hear whispered, proclaim upon the housetops" (Matthew 10:27).

Although they ask out of gracious interest, Lord,
I listen with a sense of personal guilt
whenever they greet me with the question:
"Are you writing another book?"

In their approach I seem to detect
something of the same implication
conveyed by those who ask rhetorically:
"What have you done for me recently?"

As if, Lord, I must be ever about the task
of earning more brownie points
in order to prove myself still creative,
like one who must father more children
or be suspected of losing his virility!

Isn't having nothing worth saying
reason enough to keep silent?
Isn't absence of inspiration
or lack of a deep inner compulsion
to share thoughts and insights
justification for not putting words onto paper?

The problem, I suspect, is an occupational hazard
faced by all who aspire to creative composition
whether they are blending sounds
into a musical tapestry,
blending pigment of many hues onto a canvas,
or soiling virgin paper with pregnant phrases.

But the crux of the dilemma, Lord,
involves still other questions:
 Is the restless, compulsive urge to create
 simply an extension of the ego?
 A desire for recognition, for achievement?
 A need to prove *to* oneself
 that one is not burned out, barren, impotent?

Or is it, instead, the Puritan work ethic, Lord,
impelling one to use each waking hour
lest the devil find tasks for idle hands?

Or is it conceivably a more noble impulse
to serve as a vehicle, a channel, an outlet
for some message you may wish transmitted
through music, form, color, verse, or prose?

For there is something truly transcendental, Lord,
in the way that art *(true* art, that is!)
can span time and space and culture
as when it evokes in us
an emotion, mood, or revelation
first felt and expressed generations ago
    by a Johann Sebastian Bach,
    a Leonardo da Vinci,
    or a Paul Bunyan.

Which raises still another question, Lord,
of all who feel summoned to create:
    how can those who seek to honor you
    avoid distorting what you'd have them say
    as ideas filter through their biased minds
    like sunlight dimmed by murky, misty clouds?

Is there a minister or artist, Lord,
who has not felt at some time in his heart
the clash between self-serving compromise
and your hard truths, unpopular with man?

Lastly, what of those annoying breaks
which daily interrupt creative work:
    the telephone appeal for free advice,
    the meeting called to face a civic crisis,
    the person who needs help and cannot wait,
    the plea to serve on yet another board?

What anger, what frustration, they arouse
as they intrude upon my solitude,
sidetracking thoughts or ideas just a-borning,
or making deadlines difficult to meet!
But then I think of Henri Nouwen's plaint
that throughout his life he found his work
constantly interrupted
until he made the discovery
that his interruptions
were his work!

    O Lord, help me recognize that those
    who interrupt me with their urgent needs
    may have more claim, in your eyes, to my time
    than any work I fancy I should do.

                    Amen.

Dare to Be Different

Do not be conformed to this world but be transformed by the renewal of your mind, that you may prove what is the will of God, what is good and acceptable and perfect (Romans 12:2). Having gifts that differ according to the grace given to us, let us use them: if prophecy, in proportion to our faith; if service, in our serving; he who teaches, in his teaching; he who exhorts, in his exhortation; he who contributes, in liberality; he who gives aid, with zeal; he who does acts of mercy, with cheerfulness (Romans 12:6-8).

When you first created Adam, Lord,
and then his helpmate, Eve
　　　(to the consternation of modern women
　　　who charge that your sequence
　　　also helped create male chauvinists!),
you put into motion a process of reproduction
so attractive, so alluring, so delightful
that the command "be ye fruitful and multiply"
not only was obeyed with alacrity and enthusiasm
but frequently even with lust!

And so today, thousands of years later,
we find planet Earth literally overrun
with some five billion persons who,
due to pressures involving economics,
    environmental ecology,
    agronomy and nutrition,
    political, social, and religious concerns,
are gradually adopting "unlife styles,"
often using emotion-arousing methods
for limiting population growth,
such as contraception, sterilization
and untherapeutic abortion.

But the staggering proliferation
of Adam and Eve's progeny, Lord,
seems less remarkable to us
than the daily evidence
of your incredible ingenuity and versatility.
For although all normal members of the human family
generally are heir to the same complement of parts—

eyes, ears, nose, mouth, torso, and limbs—
the variations in their size, shape, proportion, and disposition
within the flesh and skeletal structure
we call the human body
is little short of astounding.
It would seem, Lord, that your celestial computer
must have been programmed biologically
to blend, synthesize, adapt, mutate, and permutate
millions upon millions of combinations.
As a result, although we see thousands of persons daily
in the course of our busy lives,
rarely do we encounter one who strongly resembles us.

For we humans come in short, medium, tall, and extra-tall;
    skinny, slender, full-bodied, and stout;
    hairless and hairy,
    stooped and erect,
    young, middle-aged, and elderly;
    brown, black, yellow, red-skinned, and white;
    narrow-eyed, wide-eyed, cross-eyed, almond-eyed,
as from your amazing genetic storehouse
these and other biological building blocks
come together in kaleidoscopic, often whimsical, patterns
until who among us, Lord, can scan your spectrum
    of humanity
(or even, perhaps, gaze into a mirror)
without acknowledging that you have indeed
a keen sense of humor!

But in addition to our physical uniqueness, Lord,
you have given each of us an equally unique configuration
of intellectual and emotional traits.
    You have made some of us introspective,
    somber, serious, shy, sensitive, secretive,
    and others outgoing,
    suave, sociable, self-confident.
    To some you have given a bored, blasé outlook
    while others have been endowed with curiosity and
    creativity.
    Some have been blessed with one, two, or five talents,
    others with fewer talents but more heart and compassion.

Again, Lord, your celestial computer
has made human personality
a singularly individual and exciting phenomenon.
Little wonder that we seldom encounter in another
our particular matrix of moods, mannerisms,
        and mental acuity.
Yet despite the amazing diversity among us
we are inextricably linked by common bonds of humanity
(which may be the greatest miracle of all!).

> For we are one but many,
> unique but similar,
> separate but related,
> free to act as we choose
> but dependent upon our neighbor
> and upon you.
> Hence within each of us resides the basis
> for understanding others and their motivation,
> for reaching out to them
> with empathy, love, and compassion
> if only we will bring ourselves to recognize
> that we all are your children
> and therefore brothers and sisters, one of another.

Now in the face of our fascinating individualism
which is your God-given gift to each of us,
we have created among us a ridiculous vogue
for conformity.
Early in life the teenager learns
through peer pressure
that to be different from the guys and gals
is to give off the wrong vibes
and to be considered
        an oddball,
        a wet blanket,
        a square!
Better to be dead
than not to belong to the in-group.

Although adults may laugh indulgently
at this adolescent striving for approval,
they themselves fall victim
to the nationwide cult of conformity.

And how, you ask, do they conform?
And to what?

Well, Lord, too often we submerge our individuality
and, in the process, lose our distinctive appearance
by rushing to conform
with the latest vogue in dress, embellishment, or style.
If beards become fashionable,
thousands of males begin cultivating beards;
if blue eye shadow becomes the rage,
or white fingernails, or a new and costly coiffure,
females from coast to coast spend hours
putting on their blue eye shadow,
or their white fingernail polish, or fixing their hair.
Let some lionized TV actor
wear an ostentatious oversized bow tie,
and within days, boys from eight to eighty
will be wearing replicas.
If blue jeans with patches
or striped pantsuits for women
are validated by Saks Fifth Avenue or Bergdorf
Goodman,
it soon will become *de rigueur* to appear in them
regardless of the view from the rear.
Fads become so regimented
and those who follow them so sheeplike
that even the differences between the sexes
can be forced into the closet
to hide beneath the label
"unisex."

Amidst all this conformity
how refreshing can be the sight
of an Indian sari or an African dashiki
on some urban American avenue!

And consider, Lord,
how often we rush intellectually to conform
with the ideas, opinions, and prejudices of the hour
often without reflection or honest thought!

How much of our so-called conversation
    about national or world affairs
    is simply a playback of the ideas
    propagated by columnists, commentators, and lobbyists!

How many of the choices we think we make
    really are subconscious responses
    to seductive advertising
    which makes conformists of us?

How many of us, Lord, chart our careers
    to conform with the demands of a corporate employer
    who requires undeviating compliance with "policy"
    as the price for advancement
    and, in the process, forces us to become "yes-men,"
    corporate automatons in gray flannel suits?

How many of us compromise our careers
    to conform with the demands of a union steward
    who stresses, above all else, union solidarity
    and blind obedience to the dictates of union bosses?

How many of us prostitute our careers
    in so-called positions of public trust
    by finding a place, like human hogs
    at some trough of special privilege,
    because "everyone is doing it"
    and "corruption is a way of life"?

And how many of us permit our neighbors
    to conform us into faceless suburbanites
    who live in identical dwellings,
    drive identical motorcars,
    belong to identical clubs and PTA's,
    and make a religion out of suburbia's trinity:
    golf, bridge, and the happy hour?

You must weep, Lord, as you watch so many of us
surrendering the blessed individuality you have given us
for a colorless, characterless, stereotyped existence!
Yet there *are* those, praise the Lord,
who reject the mass-produced mentality of conformity
and, like the artists and craftsmen they are,
dare to be different.

These are the interesting people,
the creative people,
the innovative people
who endeavor to transform the world in which they live
and in the process often become regarded
    as oddballs,
    people out-of-step,
    unorthodox dreamers,
    impractical idealists,
    and sometimes, let us face it,
    a bit crazy!

Who are some of these crazies
whose selfless living and trust in God
have helped transform our world?

Among those within our living memory
we think of:
    Mother Teresa,
    Martin Luther King, Jr.,
    Dag Hammerskjöld,
    Teilhard de Chardin,
    Mahatma Gandhi,
    Dietrich Bonhoeffer,
    Pope John XXIII,
    Jane Addams,
    Marie Curie,
    Albert Schweitzer,
    Albert Einstein,
and, taking a great leap backward through time,
the incomparable
Jesus, the Christ.

So give us the courage, Lord,
to dare to be different.
Give us the stamina
to overcome discouragement, derision, and doubt.
Give us the faith
to "be transformed by the renewal of your mind,
that you may prove what is the will of God,
what is good and acceptable and perfect"

And through it all
help us to become
fools for Christ's sake.

Amen.

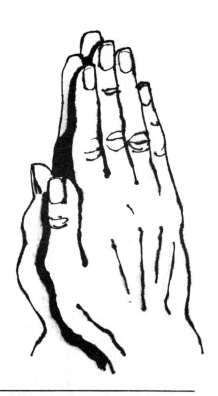

Why Pray?

"And when you pray, you must not be like the hypocrites; for they love to stand and pray in the synagogues and at the street corners, that they may be seen by men. Truly, I say to you, they have received their reward. But when you pray, go into your room and shut the door and pray to your Father who is in secret; and your Father who sees in secret will reward you. And in praying do not heap up empty phrases as the Gentiles do; for they think that they will be heard for their many words. Do not be like them, for your Father knows what you need before you ask him" (Matthew 6:5-8).

As is our custom, Lord, we had begun the weekend retreat
with a brief period of prayer,
prayer that all members of the group
might open themselves to one another
and to you
so that through the sharing of insights and concerns
we all might grow in understanding and compassion.

For those whose lives had lost meaning
we prayed for rekindled hope, vision, and renewal,
and for those whose feet were firmly on the pilgrim's path

we prayed for guidance
to new thresholds of Christian maturity.

Scarcely had we finished when a young minister in the group,
shaking his head dejectedly,
said with more than a trace of annoyance:
"This procedure of bowing our heads and praying
really makes me feel most uncomfortable.
It seems so artificial, so stagey,
to assume an attitude of prayer
and go through the motions of telling God
what we want from him.
Doesn't he already know? Do we have to tell him?
I just can't put myself in the proper mood.
I'm sorry to speak in this way, but that's how I feel."

Although we were disturbed, Lord, to hear this young cleric
express doubts and disbelief in the power of prayer,
we were grateful that he felt he could speak
with such frankness.
But how is it that a minister of the gospel
lacks faith in an act so basic to Christian belief?
Lay persons frequently express doubts of this sort,
but rarely do we hear such a statement from a pastor!

No doubt, Lord, his motivation is complex.
Some of his skepticism could reflect frustrations
arising in his parish ministry
for which his seminary training failed to prepare him.
After all, the study of Greek, Hebrew, and Aramaic texts
does little to equip a young cleric
to handle with diplomacy
a crisis such as a battle for power
in the women's society!
So if, on occasion, members of the clergy
become discouraged over *their* unanswered prayer,
what can we say in reply, Lord?
What would *you* say to us, and to them,
if only we had the grace to listen?

First, you might remind us that Jesus himself
when facing his greatest temptations and doubts
obediently turned to you in prayer.

Even during his final forlorn moments upon the cross,
forsaken and humiliated,
he cried out to you in agonizing despair.
    If this man, your Son, so free of guilt or guile,
    could place his trust in you,
    dare we imperfect, sinning mortals do less?
    Dare we declare ourselves independent
    and self-sufficient
    by making no effort to communicate with you?

For prayer is a unique form of communication
—difficult, elusive, cryptic, mysterious—
which perhaps we may begin to grasp
through an analogy,
an imperfect analogy, as indeed all analogies are,
but one we hope is an aid to our comprehension.

Visualize, if you will, a triangle.

At one of the three angles or "corners"
    each one of us exists
    along with our repository
    of thoughts, reflections, and memories,
    consciously and subconsciously sensitive
    to all the stimuli we see, hear, taste,
    touch, feel, or otherwise sense.

At a second corner of the triangle
    you, God, are dwelling—
    attentively, thoughtfully, transcendentally—
    a silent but sympathetic observer of all that we do.

And at the third corner or angle we find,
day-by-day, hour-by-hour, minute-by-minute
    all the persons, situations, and events we encounter
    as the fleeting present swiftly passes,
    leaving behind a newly lived past
    and ahead, an imminent but unknown future.

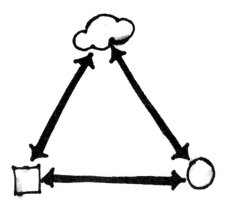

This, then, is a crude "picture" of our personal universe
through the analogy of a geometric triangle,
a triangle linking us
with all the personalities we encounter
on planet Earth
and, simultaneously, with you.

Now always among us are cynics who say:
"Yes, we can see the persons we encounter,
those at one point of your theoretical triangle,
but we cannot see God at the other point;
indeed, we cannot see him because he doesn't exist!"

This seems like a rather brash attitude,
doesn't it, Lord,
in view of our abysmal ignorance about the true extent
of your vast and, to us, incomprehensible universe!

These cynics appear to be living
under a spiritual cloud cover,
accepting the blessings of the warm, friendly rays
which filter through to them
but not choosing to ascend in their thinking
to a height where they can sense the actual presence
of a supreme life-sustaining power.
Yet we must recognize that today
we all see through the clouds darkly,
but one day, face-to-face!

Shall we continue, Lord, with our geometric analogy?

We encounter those at one corner of the triangle
as a result of our, or their, volition.
Either we choose the persons, events, or places
we will be exposed to
or the persons, events, or places intrude upon our lives.

In either case, we find ourselves in communication
through the spoken or written word,
through facial expressions, gestures, physical contacts,
or, sometimes, through flashes of recognition or intuition
we are unable fully to understand, much less explain.

But how do you, Lord, from your invisible location
at the third corner of our triangle,
convey your thoughts and ideas to us?
  How do we convey our concerns and needs to you?
  How do we find you, and how do you find us?
  How do we penetrate the cloud cover
  that makes recognition and identification so difficult?

Let us pause a moment to acknowledge that if you, Lord,
are indeed a "third-party"
to all our contacts with those persons
at the "second corner" of our living triangle
and if we become truly sensitive to this relationship,
then every aspect of our life can become prayer-full
and you will strongly influence the whole of living.

In other words, we will be constantly linked with you—
    aware of your invisible presence,
    influenced by your guiding hand,
    sustained by your love,
    restrained by subtle stirrings within us
    throughout every interpersonal situation we experience.
Now if our communication with those we see
takes many forms,
how natural that we communicate with you, too,
in a variety of ways.
Sometimes we will communicate with you silently
as thoughts and needs and petitions flash through our minds.
Sometimes the contact will be verbal
as the act of putting our problem into words
helps us to define the situation we face,
sort out the component parts,
see them more clearly,
then appeal to you for understanding and strength.
Sometimes, as in earthly communication,
we will speak on our own behalf,
    expressing gratitude to you,
    asking forgiveness of you,
    acknowledging our dependence upon you,
    soliciting your help in a specific area of concern.

Often, however, we will find ourselves
interceding for others,
asking your help, your power, your mercy
to make another's problems more bearable, more solvable.
Although these petitions of ours may be private,
often they will be spoken in public
as we seek to gather up the concerns of a group
and bring them to you on their behalf.
It was this sort of communication at our retreat, Lord,
which so disturbed our young minister friend
who apparently resented the "programmed" aspect
of corporate prayer.

    But turning to what is, for many people,
    the most perplexing problem of prayer,
    we raise the mind-boggling question:
    how do you communicate with us, Lord?

Too often it seems to us
that you are like some far-off telephone-answering device
which invites us to record our messages following the
    "beep"
but only hints that at some later time
you *may* return the call,
in what form, we haven't the slightest idea!

We ourselves must acknowledge, Lord,
that any answer requires patience on our part,
faith in your ultimate concern for us,
and above all, a willingness to listen
sensitively, imaginatively, trustingly.

On rare occasions we may actually hear you speaking to us
in a vision, in a dream, in a flash of insight
much as Ananias heard you instruct him to call on Saul
and be instrumental in converting him to Christianity.
Or we may feel a compelling urge to take some action
we would not normally consider taking; for example,
picking up a phone impulsively
and calling a neglected friend
and hearing that person exclaim:

    "Thank God!
    I was hoping you or someone might call.
    I'm in serious trouble and need help!"
    (Which suggests that you, God, may call on *us*
    to be the blessed answer
    to someone *else's* fervent prayer!)

Or we may feel an inexplicable urge *not* to take
some long-contemplated action
and later ponder why
we were thus spared some distressing consequence.

Or we find some person or event entering our lives
and making such a difference that we call it a "coincidence,"
not pausing to ask if the coincidence
might have been divinely inspired.

Or we expose ourselves to great music,
great art, great drama,
or participate in an inspiring service of worship
and suddenly feel the air cleared
of doubt and uncertainty
as a fresh direction providentially emerges.

And how often, Lord, you choose to speak to us
through the words of those we daily encounter,
    words of encouragement which cheer us on,
    words of caution which alert us to danger,
    words of sympathy which soften our grief,
    words of criticism which help us understand
    our real selves.

And how frequently, Lord, you send us your Holy Spirit
where two, three, or more of us gather in your name,
and in ways we cannot understand
but are grateful for
we feel your presence dwelling in our midst!

    Now having pondered some aspects of prayer,
    where in all this is Jesus, the Christ?
    What is his role in our prayer lives?
    How does he relate to you, God,
    and to us as well?
    Do we worship Christ or do we worship you?

Since these have been perplexing problems
for many of us, Lord,
let's take a final moment or two
and try to sort out some of the angles
of that theological triangle called the Trinity!

First, we are eternally grateful to you, God,
for the gift of your Son, Jesus,
without whom we might find it impossible
ever to establish a relationship with you.

For behind that veil of clouds
in the third corner of our allegorical triangle
you are an unseen deity
whose omnipotence is supreme.
Yet we have faith that you are not a hostile monarch
spying on us with vengeful wrath
but, instead, like an earthly father and mother
who watch us with love and compassion,
waiting patiently as we fend for ourselves
but instantly available in time of need.

We know this, and have this faith today,
because some two thousand years ago
there dwelt in that second corner of our triangle
a flesh and blood man named Jesus
with whom we can identify today—
	a man, like us, who was tempted,
	a man, like us, who knew pain and sorrow,
	a man, like us, who enjoyed a party,
	a man, like us, who turned to you in prayer.

Yet this flesh and blood man, so like us,
developed that spark of divinity we all inherit
into a glowing, incandescent light of the world
through his perfect obedience to you,
his subordination of ego to the needs of others,
his refusal to retaliate and perpetuate hatred and strife,
and his supreme sacrifice for us on the cross.

	Because you so loved the world,
	you gave us this unique man
	in whom we can glimpse you
	as the invisible becomes, in him, visible.

And today, through your gift of the Holy Spirit,
we discover the living Christ
wherever we mortals create the climate
of brotherhood, self-sacrifice, love, and reconciliation.

And so when we pray to you, God, it is in Christ's name
in grateful acknowledgment that we come to you
through your Son, the Christ,
    the translator,
    the interpreter,
    the man-God link
who not only has made you accessible to us
but who is also our intermediary and Savior.

                Amen.

Care Package

He said also to the man who had invited him, "When you give a dinner or a banquet, do not invite your friends or your brothers or your kinsmen or rich neighbors, lest they also invite you in return, and you be repaid. But when you give a feast, invite the poor, the maimed, the lame, the blind, and you will be blessed, because they cannot repay you. You will be repaid at the resurrection of the just" (Luke 14:12-14).

It was a long and frustrating strike,
and if you were present at the bargaining table, Lord,
the negotiators for both company and union
seemed unaware of your presence.

Each morning those of us who were managers
or technical specialists
or confidential secretaries
or employees exempt for other reasons
drove slowly into the company's parking lots,
passing protesting pickets who stared at us
    defiantly,
    belligerently,
    sullenly,
    or with a weary sadness.

Once inside the prisonlike confines of the plant
we went about unfamiliar tasks
aimed at maintaining some semblance of production
so that the essential needs of important customers
could be partially met.

And as the days relentlessly grew into weeks
and weeks stretched into months,
the tension between the "insiders"
and all those outside the corporate compound
steadily built up.

We who were manning the machines
began to feel subtly sanctimonious
as we contrasted our labor and our loyalty
with the greed, arrogance, and stubbornness
of the union-led renegades outside,
while those shuffling on the picket line,
often in windy wintry weather,
worried about the growing pile of unpaid bills
and cursed the company, their creditors, and us.

And so our basic humanity swiftly eroded
as the adversaries were stripped
of their personal identities
and became, instead, impersonal stereotypes:
   strikers and pickets, on the one hand,
   union-busters, scabs, and company stooges,
      on the other.

Sad to relate, we found ourselves grimly reenacting
the classic pattern of economic warfare:
   the besiegers, striving to isolate the enemy
      by cutting off supplies to the combat zone,
      by enlisting other unions in a boycott,
      by threatening with violence those still working;
   the defenders, seeking to outflank the attackers
      by obtaining injunctions and restraining orders,
      by firing barrages of press releases,
      by placing a strain on the union's strike fund.

But suddenly, Lord, in the midst of all this strife
a postal truck breached the picket line
to deliver a large brown carton
addressed to one of the corporate department heads.
For some time it was regarded with apprehension,
gently shaken, listened to, carefully scrutinized
as one might handle a suspected time bomb.

Finally the stout twine was severed
and cautiously, gingerly, the parcel was opened.
From inside emerged a festively wrapped package
replete with ribbon, bow, and gift card
which read:

   "To my dear friends and coworkers
   I send this care package
   with assurance of my love and affection."
   It was simply signed, "Alice."

No further identification was needed,
for everyone still working in the department
immediately recognized the sender,
a warmhearted, popular young woman
whose vocation was that of computer programmer.

Slices of the chocolate layer cake she had sent
along with some of her homemade cookies
soon were circulating throughout the department,
while by courier and inside telephone
word of the gift from "the enemy"
speedily traveled to the farthermost reaches
of the strikebound plant.

Smiles replaced frowns;
surprise gave way to delight
as tensions suddenly relaxed.
    "Alice may not live here anymore,"
    but her friendly, compassionate spirit
    was spreading warmth to the coldest hearts.
        Someone cared,
        even among the pickets,
        and it made a difference.

Lord, you care for us like that!
When the going becomes rough
and we feel forlorn and forsaken,
suddenly your Spirit breaks through
and warms our hearts
even though we may be undeserving of your love.

    When was the last time, Lord, that
    we sent a care package to someone in need?

77

Christ urges us to love our enemies
which is hard to do, even if we have the desire,
for "love" is an emotion which takes not just time
but also intimate knowledge and repeated contacts
and cannot be turned on at our whim.

But in his admonition to invite to our table
not merely friends and brothers and neighbors
who can invite us in return
but, instead, the poor, the maimed, the lame, the blind,
Christ is urging us to *care* for unlovely, unloved people,
people like us in the strikebound plant.

Social psychologists tell us that attractive folk—
those with good looks, good manners,
outgoing personalities, all the amenities—
have few difficulties and encounter few obstacles
in attaining their goals in life.

> These are the "successful" people,
> the charmers who are welcome at any banquet table.

But what of those we meet who are unlovely:
the reticent, the resentful, the rebellious,
the homely, the handicapped, the habitual losers,
those maimed in mind, body, or spirit?

> How hungry *they* must be, Lord, for a care package!
> Or how they must long for an invitation
> to someone's banquet table!

Banquet table, care package—
> aren't these symbols of two ways
in which we can become caring persons?
If we are open, receptive, and understanding,
a person in need may respond to our hospitality
and join us at our table,
> wherever, and in whatever form,
> that table may exist.

Or if we are compassionate enough to sense another's need,
we may reach out to that person
and offer our special care package:

> a material package of food, clothing, or shelter;
> an emotional package of listening intently,
> identifying with, affirming, and supporting;
> a spiritual package of helping a troubled soul
> through the difficult, often painful process
> of finding the real self, coming to terms with life,
> and accepting the gift of your forgiveness.

Thank you, Lord, for all of your dedicated followers
who daily perform this sort of caring
in our complex, sophisticated society.

> We think not only of the men and women
>   of the Salvation Army
> who provide food, shelter, and spiritual uplift
> for the maimed souls who come to their table,
> but also of
> groups like "Meals on Wheels"
> which reach out to the elderly and infirm
> bringing care packages of food and friendliness.

> We think not only of physicians, surgeons,
> and hospital volunteers
> who day-in, day-out, provide skilled medical care
> for those who come seeking healing,
> but also of
> the ingenious visiting nurses
> whose care package is a compact medical kit
> and a warm heart.

We think not only of scoutmasters, "Y" leaders, and social workers
who bring girls and boys into a supportive fellowship
but also of
Big Brothers and Big Sisters
who reach out to provide guidance and encouragement
for youngsters at life's crossroads.

We think of the countless religious congregations
which bring lost sheep to *their* tables
and the many ministers, counselors, and therapists
who spend long, difficult hours reaching out
to the maladjusted,
to the mentally disturbed,
to the spiritually maimed.

And what of those of us who are called to be lay ministers?
Where do *we* fit into your scheme of things, Lord?
How do we set up our special tables of hospitality,
put together our special care packages?
Doesn't it require of us, Lord,
that we not only be available to people
at the time and place of their need
but that we also cultivate the art
of sensitizing ourselves to their moods?
How can we ever empathize with others
if we are unable to relate to their innermost feelings?

Too often we resemble the actor or actress who,
failing to "get inside" the character being portrayed,
gives a hollow, lifeless, unconvincing performance.
Only when the thespian breaks away from familiar
surroundings
and for a time actually lives amidst similar characters
feeling their emotions,
suffering their hurts,
experiencing their hopes, fears, and doubts
does the performer breathe life into the role.

Wasn't much of the charisma of Jesus
a result of his amazing power
to understand more about the people he encountered
than they understood about themselves
so that with a rare compassion
he could share and bear their suffering?

Help us, Lord,
to feel something of *his* joy and pain
as we struggle to care deeply for others,
for that. indeed, is the "secret"
of the incarnation.

Amen.

Wailing Wall

I appeal to you, brethren, by the name of our Lord Jesus Christ, that all of you agree and that there be no dissensions among you, but that you be united in the same mind and the same judgment (1 Corinthians 1:10).

For as in one body we have many members and all the members do not have the same function, so we, though many, are one body in Christ, and individually members one of another. . . . Let love be genuine; hate what is evil, hold fast to what is good; love one another with brotherly affection; outdo one another in showing honor (Romans 12:4-5, 9-10).

So with yourselves; since you are eager for manifestations of the Spirit, strive to excel in building up the church (1 Corinthians 14:12).

For three consecutive Sundays, Lord,
I haven't seen them in church.
Although such an absence by some other members
would not occasion so much as a raised eyebrow,
it becomes disturbingly noticeable
in the case of the Johnsons
who invariably occupy the same pew,
smile and nod to the same people,
leave the church by the same door,

and bid adieu to the senior minister
by telling him in the same modulated voice
how much they enjoyed the sermon
(although Herb Johnson has been heard to mutter testily:
"It was too damned long!").

I am certain, Lord, that they aren't out of town,
and I know that they aren't ill,
for Herb has been seen on the golf course
and Janice has attended the weekly meetings
of the Women's Civic Club.

> "Oh, dear, what can the matter be?
> Oh, dear, what can the matter be?
> Oh, dear, what can the matter be?
> The Johnsons are absent from church!"

Could they, like the Millers, have taken offense
at something Pastor Wilkinson said in a sermon?
Or were they, like the Stevensons, upset
because the editor of the church newsletter
omitted their names from the list
of those contributing altar flowers at Eastertime?
Or did they think it a sacrilege, several Sundays ago,
when the choir sang music from *Godspell?*
Or is Herb annoyed at being dropped from the council
in spite of having missed seven consecutive meetings?

Lord, I've received no letter of complaint
from either of the Johnsons,
> no phone calls,
> no personal entreaties,
> no rumors of unrest conveyed to me by a third party
as is often the case
when church members become disenchanted;
for, Lord, I am the church's Lay Leader
which makes of me a wailing wall
for the distressed, the disturbed, the disillusioned.

They descend upon me
> sometimes with tears in their eyes,
> sometimes with despair in their voices,
> sometimes with indignation flushing their countenances
as they acquaint me with real or fancied hurts

they choose not to tell the ministers,
for they know, Lord, that I have become
the church's paracleric.

> But surely they don't expect *me*
> to cast out demons!
> Or do they?

In the 1960s, Lord, my task was especially onerous
as I found myself the target of angry letters
sometimes signed by several parishioners
to give them a petition-like urgency.

Why were our ministers opposing the Vietnam war
and displaying a disgraceful lack of patriotism?
How dare they express sympathy for draft evaders—
those spineless, yellow-bellied refugees
from military service?
Why were members of our church permitted
to march in the South with civil rights agitators
when already the blacks were becoming too pushy,
too impatient in spite of rapid progress?
By what right did the church sanction civil disobedience
when most of its members were law-abiding citizens?
And why did we permit our church school building
to become an overnight dormitory
for members of that rabble—the Poor People's March—
on their way to demonstrate in our nation's capital?

These and other emotion-laden issues of the sixties
turned loose the serpent
in our ecclesiastical Garden of Eden,
provoking dissension instead of discussion,
combativeness instead of conciliation,
alienation instead of accommodation.

> Yes, Lord, it is infinitely easier
> to compromise our Christian values
> into conformity with this distorted culture of ours
> than to strive to reshape that culture
> into closer conformity with the values
> for which Christ lived and died!

And so today, as we have settled back slothfully
into a more conservative and less activist posture
(although we still sturdily maintain
we are true disciples of Christ!),
the tensions and trauma of the sixties
have subsided.

> Yet we still witness the spectacle
> of the Johnsons and the Millers and the Stevensons
> beating their fists on the wailing wall
> as they find within the church family
> countless sources of petty annoyance.

> Why, Lord? Why?

Does it reflect the gnawing fear
that our lives are slipping beyond our control
as the tempo of technological change
whirls faster and faster,
confronting us with new and perplexing problems—
> the specter of unemployment amidst prosperity,
> the grave depletion of natural resources,
> the erosion of purchasing power by inflation,
> the fears of spreading nuclear technology,
> the perils of overpopulation,
> the desecration of our environment,
> the demonic possibilities inherent
> in genetic engineering—
causing us to yearn for escape
and a return to the fancied peace and tranquillity
of a Walden-like existence
and what many nostalgically associate with it,
the little church in the wildwood?

Or does it reflect, Lord, an unrealistic expectation
that the church should be "a fellowship of saints,"
a place where there is no false pride,
no jealousy, no envy,
no hypocrisy,
in fact, none of the sorry human traits
that qualify the best of us
to be called "sinner"?

Yet Jesus, upon hearing the Pharisees
ask of his disciples,
"Why does your teacher eat with tax collectors
and sinners?"
said to them,
> "Those who are well have no need of a physician,
> but those who are sick.
> Go and learn what this means,
> 'I desire mercy, and not sacrifice.'
> For I came not to call the righteous,
> but sinners."

Or does the disenchantment of the Johnsons
reflect, instead, a cynical distrust of authority,
brought about by the crass misuse of power
    in high places in our government,
    in paneled corporate board rooms,
    in grubby union meeting halls,
leading many church people
to view with subconscious suspicion
the authority of pastor, priest, or rabbi?

For just as a teacher
confronts a student with challenges,
correcting his errors and prodding his lagging thoughts,
so our spiritual mentor confronts us
with the need to reorder our lives
and in the process becomes, in the eyes of some,
a father-figure they subconsciously—
with Freudian intensity—
resolve to resist, to challenge, to oppose.

    (And when a senior minister is cast
    in the role of father-image,
    who, you ask, becomes the mother-image?
    Who but the young associate,
    the object of sympathy, love, and affection!)

Or does the unhappiness of the Johnsons
reflect simply their plaintive plea for attention—
a plea from persons swallowed up
by the world's inhumanity,
weary of the daily struggle for status,
fearful of the threat of self-knowledge,
and wanting only to be clasped in a warm embrace
by their father-mother God
and to be told that they are loved, protected, and secure?

And if the Johnsons do drift away, Lord,
will it be because of the delicate fragility
of the bonds which hold together the family in Christ?
Will it reflect their lack of deep commitment,
their lack of patience with others in the family,
their inability to see the divine spark
in all of God's children
regardless of race, age, income, or culture?

Or does it reflect *our* failure, Lord,
to create the kind of intimate climate
in which all members of the body of Christ
are warmly welcomed, warts and all,
    without reservation,
    without judgment,
    without equivocation?

Lord, may all of us who serve your church,
whether as deacons, elders, stewards, or lay leaders
strive to help our fellowship become
a microcosm of the ultimate good society.

A society where each and every member is valued
    for his or her unique personhood;
a society so inclusive, so colorful, so diverse
    that all within it gain strength and wisdom
    and are enriched
    by its many-splendored diversity;
a society without regimentation of thought, word, or belief
    but only a common dedication
    to the vision Christ gives us of you;
a society which provides us with ample *Lebensraum*
    for our personal pilgrimage through life
    so that each may grow in understanding and maturity
    through the pain of honest doubt,
    the stimulation of learning,
    the excitement of discovery,
    the joy of self-realization,
    the ecstasy of actually experiencing
    the Holy Spirit in our midst;

a society which lives purposefully and not aimlessly
   by striving to win for all people
   justice tempered with mercy,
   freedom accompanied by responsibility,
   opportunity unhampered by prejudice,
   respect freely given and gratefully received.

And if all this appears overwhelming
or so idealistic as to seem unattainable,
let each of us start with the Johnsons
in our church families
and vow to win back the lost sheep.

And how do we spot the sheep
who are just beginning to stray?
One significant symptom:
   their reference to the church—
   its ministers, its mentors, its members—
   as "they" instead of "we."

But what if our efforts at reconciliation
meet with antagonism?
   Rebelliousness?
      Even anger?

Then, Lord, help us to meet the Christian challenge
   by loving the hell
      out of them!

                                   Amen.

The Scripture quoted in the text of this prayer
is found in Matthew 9:12-13.

The Popular Art of Manipulation

These are grumblers, malcontents, following their own passions, loud-mouthed boasters, flattering people to gain advantage (Jude 16).

> Do not boast about tomorrow,
>   for you do not know what a day
>   may bring forth.
> Let another praise you, and not your
>   own mouth;
>   a stranger, and not your own lips.
>   (Proverbs 27:1-2)

Therefore you have no excuse, O man, whoever you are, when you judge another; for in passing judgment upon him you condemn yourself, because you, the judge, are doing the very same things (Romans 2:1).

The guests on the TV late show, Lord,
provide an interesting display of exhibitionism
as they emerge from the backdrop
to be greeted by the genial host
and the expectant audience.

Some are extremely aggressive
as, with a real or feigned air of self-assurance,
they come charging onto the stage,

plop down into the guest chair,
and seize the initiative
by boldly proclaiming their identity,
immodestly describing their most recent triumphs,
and striving to dominate the interview
by regaling the audience with their opinions
on topics calculated to show them off to advantage.

Others, more subtle, step out quietly,
take their place in the guest chair,
smile ingratiatingly
and wait for the host to set the tempo
with his words of welcome and opening remarks.
But seldom does this more relaxed approach
indicate a retiring or withdrawn personality!
For these guests frequently are expert
at watching and waiting, cobra-like,
for an opportunity to strike at any opening
and place their host on the defensive.
Once the host has become the victim of the attack,
the guest moves in with calm competence,
    deadly dispatch,
    and precise phrasing
to make the points he or she came on the show
specifically to make.

Still other guests have mastered the art of the taciturn
by emerging hesitatingly from the rear waiting area,
sinking uneasily into the guest chair,
and confronting the host with a blank stare accompanied by
silence
and by all the outward signs of stage fright,
shyness, and embarrassment.
In response to questions, these characters intone
a monosyllabic "yes" or "no."

By their facial expressions, actions, and laconic answers,
they seek to convey the impression
that their participation is reluctant,
their presence an inconvenience,
and their exposure to the audience almost distasteful.

But let the host refer to something they desire to promote—
    a forthcoming appearance at a supper club,
    a recently recorded album,
    or a newly published book—
and they miraculously come to life,
become voluble, almost animated,
and eagerly volunteer information
calculated to stimulate interest
in whatever they are promoting.

But some of the fastest, most glib chatter
and the most contrived display of enthusiasm
are encountered when the guest is an author
whose appearance has been artfully arranged
by his or her agent or publisher.
The sort of slick maneuvering that takes place
perhaps can be best illustrated
by the case of the young and wide-eyed damsel who,
after holding forth at great length about her book,
suddenly paused, looked contrite, and exclaimed
almost penitently:
    "But here, I've been talking entirely too much
    about myself.
    Let's talk, instead,
    about *you!*"
    And then, with an eager and inviting smile:
    "What do *you* think of my book?"

Whenever we encounter such obvious manipulation, Lord,
we feel disgust and annoyance
not merely at the persons themselves
and their contrived showmanship
but also at the basic idea of plotting deception
in an effort to profit at our expense.
We are human enough, Lord, to resent efforts
to "take us in."
In fact, each time I am the victim of manipulation,
I find myself
deploring the duplicity, the deviousness,
mistrusting the maneuvering,
becoming enraged at the exploitation,
resenting the . . .

But wait, Lord!
Why is my irritation so strident?
Why am I overreacting?
Displaying self-righteousness?
Becoming so judgmental?

Is it because I resent in others
what I fear in myself?
Am I, myself, guilty of manipulation
whenever I am introduced to others,
not on the late show
where I might conceivably have an excuse,
but in everyday life
when I meet for the first time
a stranger?

How often do I deliberately seek to make an impression
by citing some real or fancied accomplishment
or by referring to some prestigious affiliation
or by resorting to the most subtle manipulation of all,
name-dropping?
And how seldom do I expend the same effort
to learn something about this new acquaintance
by asking a few sincere questions,
by inviting this person to reveal who he or she is
so that I might savor the uniqueness
of a potential friend!

How much precious energy we waste, Lord,
and how much frustration we cause
by practicing the popular art of manipulation!

Who among us has not, at some time,
made a calculated use of flattery
to get what we want from someone in power?

Who among us has not withheld
some sought-for favor, privilege, or right—
an introduction, a promotion, a financial reward,
a gift, an outing, even marital sex—
as a weapon to force
compliance with our wishes?

Who among us has not used the device
of publicly asking an unanswerable question
in order to embarrass and "put someone down"?

Who among us has not manipulated another
through the "bargaining" technique
of seeking advantage by dangling a lure
before the eyes of our perplexed victim?
"If you do what I want you to do,
I will give you all this!"
(reminiscent of the technique used by the devil
in tempting your Son
by promising the world
in exchange for his soul).

> These, Father, constitute sins,
> sometimes trivial, sometimes grave,
> insofar as they use fear, flattery,
> force, or fabrication
> to deprive another of freedom of choice,
> manipulating that person in such a way
> as to make him or her our pawn.

And finally, Lord, how great is our need for forgiveness
when we use manipulation,
Machiavellian-like,
ostensibly to advance your kingdom
because we glibly feel that such a laudable end
justifies any means.

We think of the subtle, and not so subtle, pressures
frequently exerted by clergy and laity alike

to maneuver persons into affiliation with their churches,
not on the basis of a creative Christian community
where the newcomer can grow in faith,
in sensitivity to human need,
and in commitment to Christ and service
to the least of your children,
but rather by offering a club-like fellowship
where little is demanded, much is promised,
and growth is measured statistically,
not theologically.

We think of shameful proselytizing
which aims to lure persons from one church to another,
from one denomination to another,
or into some pseudoreligious sect
which worships not you
but its self-serving, self-anointed guru.

Above all else, Lord,
help us to respect those of other faiths
    so that we may maintain a meaningful dialogue
    with our Jewish brothers and sisters
    without threatening their integrity or ours,
    open to our mutual love for the one God,
    respectful of our sacred traditions,
    so that together we may enrich
    each other's understanding
      and in the process become
      better Christians and Jews.

                Amen.

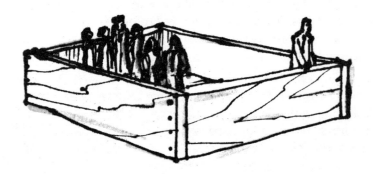

So You're Not Religious!

"Not everyone who says to me, 'Lord, Lord,' shall enter the kingdom of heaven, but he who does the will of my father who is in heaven. On that day many will say to me, 'Lord, Lord, did we not prophesy in your name, and cast out demons in your name, and do mighty works in your name?' And then will I declare to them, 'I never knew you; depart from me, you evildoers'" (Matthew 7:21-23).

"I'm not a religious person," writes a newspaper columnist,
although the content of his journalistic essays
and his frequent appearances on a TV news commentary
clearly show him to be a man of high ideals,
of compassion,
and of concern for people and their problems.

How often we meet persons face-to-face
who express that same thought,
     some apologetically,
     others indifferently,
     still others with an ill-concealed air of defiance!

What they really are saying is:
"I have no meaningful connection with organized religion.
I don't belong to a parish.
I don't attend church.
Therefore I am looked upon by most churchgoers
as a sinner, an outcast, a heathen."

All of which, Lord, raises some potentially perplexing
    questions:
Does membership in a church signify that a person is religious?
Conversely, does nonmembership brand one as unreligious?
Do you, God, write a celestial insurance policy for the
    churched
but deny protection from hell fire to the unchurched?
Are those within a church family "saints"
and those on the outside "sinners"?

Now one suspects that church members and nonmembers
might give very different answers to these questions.
But of more concern, Lord, is trying to find
your answers to what many consider a dilemma.

At the outset perhaps we can examine
what might be called the "marks of religious persons":
namely, seven attitudes or beliefs
which are not exclusively Christian
but which seem characteristic
of most truly religious individuals.

First and foremost, Lord, is a belief in you,
a faith or conviction that you exist
even though your existence cannot be proved.
>That this belief is widespread is borne out by surveys
>revealing that few of us are atheists or agnostics.
>And even many of those who doubt your existence
>turn to you in desperation
>when caught in the foxholes of life.

A second mark of religious persons
is their realization, Lord, that you give meaning to life
that otherwise would lack depth, breadth, and ultimate value.
>Human beings want and need to feel
>>that a power greater and more awesome than their puny
>>>selves
>transcends, illumines, undergirds, and authenticates
>their earthly existences.
>Why, Lord, are we intrigued by mystery stories created
>>by human minds?
>Is it because you are the ultimate mystery
>whom we yearn to know and comprehend
>so that our incomplete lives may become complete,
>our imperfect lives more perfect,
>our finite lives infinite?

A third mark of religious persons
is their appreciation that you, Lord, are the God of history;
    that in you we have an overarching timeless link
    with the past and our roots in your act of creation,
    with the present and the challenges you place before us,
    and with the future and our upward climb
    toward what Teilhard de Chardin has called "omega,"
    your destiny for us in reunion with you.

A fourth mark of religious persons
is their deeply felt urge to worship you
    in awe of your omnipotence,
    in gratitude for your vast creation,
    and with reverence for your holiness.

A fifth mark of religious persons
is their awareness that through prayer
we have a channel of communication with you
    and that earnest prayer can have a profound effect
    on our spiritual vitality and all we seek to do,
    on others for whom we pray,
    and on you, who are always ready to listen.

A sixth mark of religious persons
is their trust in your eternal goodness
    in your benevolence and mercy,
    and in your concern for humanity.

And the seventh mark of religious persons
is their belief that we all are your children
    and that we express our love for you
    by loving our brothers and sisters
    wherever we may encounter them in our daily living.
    For you *are* the Lord of all men and women—
    Christians, Jews, Muslims, Buddhists—
    and to you turn all who profess a faith
    in one supreme God, the parent of all humankind.

Now to these seven basic beliefs
Christians add four—
four that are vitally important
to their beliefs and their avowed style of life.

The first—and basic to all the rest—
is the conviction that in Jesus Christ,
your unique gift to us,
    we see you embodied in a human being
    who, by living among persons and sharing their burdens,
    enables us to comprehend what it means to be godlike.

The second mark of religious Christians
is their gratitude for the Good News,
    the exciting word that Christ,
    by his sacrifice on the cross
    and his subsequent resurrection,
    gave his sinless life to save our sinful selves
    so that all who believe may be pardoned
    and have the promise of life everlasting.

The third mark of religious Christians
is their understanding that belief in Christ
calls for imitating Christ,
    striving to live with something of his love and compassion
    through service to others
    and sharing the Good News with them.

And the fourth mark of religious Christians
is their recognition that the church founded by Peter and by
       Paul
—much as Christ and his disciples gathered in the upper
       room—
is today the fellowship of believers
    essential to the preserving and propagating of the faith,
    vitally important for worship, mutual support,
    and the fostering of community,
    and invaluable as the center from which must radiate
    service to all whom Christ would have us help.

Now it is this fourth mark of Christians, Lord,
—the centrality of the church to the faith—
which seems to be most misunderstood by the churched and
       the unchurched
and the cause of dissension between the two.

"I can be a perfectly good Christian
without ever darkening the door of a church,"
proclaims the unchurched person defiantly,
failing to recognize how difficult it is
to be a member of the family of Christ
in detached service.

    "If you're not a regular churchgoer,
    you're a lost soul, a sinner,
    and you'll never win God's forgiveness,"
    retorts the church person piously,
    blithely overlooking the tepid quality of church
       membership
    and lack of earnest commitment
    on the part of so many within the congregation.

"The people inside our churches
are escapees from the trials of the world,"
argue the unchurched caustically.
"They take refuge in their hymns and prayers
and, keeping their hands unsoiled by the riffraff,
watch unconcernedly from their ecclesiastical fortresses
while the world plummets to hell!"

"It's easy to criticize from the outside,"
reminds the churchgoer plaintively,
"but much harder to join us and work for salvation.
After all, we have earned favor in God's sight
by virtue of our virtue!"
(Such smugness is summed up in the incredible phrase:
"I own a piece of the cross,"
a slogan which may paraphrase the Prudential
but certainly is not providential!)

Distorted as these views are, Lord,
there is enough truth in them
to confront us all,
churched and unchurched alike,
with your judgment
and, we hope,
also with your mercy.

Forgive all of us within the church, Lord,
who feel we are among the elite,
possessors of special privilege
and therefore free of sin!

Forgive all of us outside the church, Lord,
who feel we don't need Christ's family,
are not hypocrites like church folk,
are intellectually superior and able to order our lives
without dogma, liturgies, creeds, and clergy!

For who among us really has accepted Christ
in the sense of fully comprehending him—
> his godliness,
> his humanity,
> his love and compassion,
> his loneliness and frustration,
> his pain and suffering,
> his obedience unto death upon the cross,
> much less embodying in our lives
> all for which he taught, lived, and died?

Even his disciples couldn't grasp his amazing grace
but deserted him in his hour of extreme anguish.
Yet a lowly criminal, suffering beside him on a cross,
glimpsed his divinity and recognized our Savior.
Was it because this criminal, this sinner, this lowly man
suffered with Christ?

> Who among us, Lord, can "earn" salvation?
> Who among us can "deserve" your favor?
> Who among us is not guilty of sin and sinning
> and therefore is not in need of forgiveness?

> We may be a chosen people,
> but never let us forget that you, Lord,
> do the choosing.

Amen.

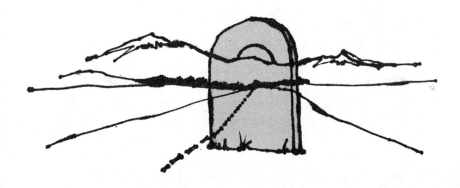

Dead End

For I know that the Lord is great,
    and that our Lord is above all gods.
Whatever the Lord pleases he does,
    in heaven and on earth,
    in the seas and all deeps.

He it is who makes the clouds rise
    at the end of the earth,
    who makes lightnings for the rain
    and brings forth the wind from his
    storehouses.

(Psalm 135:5-7)

For God so loved the world that he gave his only Son, that whoever believes
in him should not perish but have eternal life. For God sent the Son into the
world, not to condemn the world, but that the world might be saved through
him (John 3:16-17).

The fool says in his heart,
    "There is no God."
    They are corrupt, they do
    abominable deeds,
    there is none that does good.
The Lord looks down from heaven
    upon the children of men,
    to see if there are any that act
    wisely,
    that seek after God.

They have all gone astray, they are
    all alike corrupt;
    there is none that does good,
    no, not one.

(Psalm 14:1-3)

Is there anyone among us, Lord,
who has not at some time
with honest anguish
asked that crucial question:
  "Are you there?
  Are you for real?
  Or are we laboring under
  a well-publicized illusion,
  fostered by sincere but misguided people,
  that this is your world
  and we are in your hands?"

We pray to you, Lord,
thanking you for gracious gifts,
but are those gifts simply
the culmination of our own strenuous efforts?

We pray to you for help and strength,
but the batting average of the results
sometimes seems barely to approximate mere chance!

We pray prayers of intercession
for those with urgent, often painful, need;
yet frequently it avails us nothing
as dread suspicions are confirmed
and all hope for loved ones is lost.

We see your beautiful, awe-filled world
suddenly become convulsed
by earthquake, tornado, avalanche, and volcanic eruption,
and we wonder about your mercy and compassion
when thousands are killed, maimed, made homeless
by forces beyond our control
but presumably at your command.

We ponder your promise of life eternal
as voiced so movingly by your Son
and celebrated by so many religions
    (although in some, life after death
    is disturbingly anonymous and amorphous!);
then we contemplate the billions upon billions of souls
who have, from the beginning of time,

plodded in an endless procession through life
from cradle to grave
and we wonder!

What super-universe of mind or matter
is so unfathomably enormous
as to encompass such a cloud of witnesses?

Lord, it boggles our imaginations
to try to conceive of such a Nirvana
from the viewpoint and limited perspective
of our earthbound embryonic intellects.
If we still can't fathom
the myriad mysteries of a universe
that we can see, hear, and touch,
how helpless we find ourselves
speculating about the nature of an existence
with which we seem to have no reference points
of time, space, form, or substance!

But then again we hear your Son's assurance
that those who believe shall have eternal life,
for in our Father's house are many rooms
and if it were not so, would he have lied?
Still more incredible is Christ himself,
humiliated, crucified with thieves,
his body sealed in a rocky tomb
and given up for dead by all who mourned
only to reappear on three occasions,
bringing such astonishment and joy
to Mary Magdalene and Christ's disciples
that modern skeptics who, like Thomas, doubt
the resurrection's authenticity
nevertheless concede that something happened,
some awesome miracle that shook the world.

We also think of those great intellects—
philosophers, religious sages, seers—
as well as folk of simple, humble faith,
who, through the centuries of human existence,
have hailed the promise of a future life
and lived creatively with hope and trust.

Why, we ask, is life so incomplete,
so finite, and so lacking in perfection?

Why is life cut short while there is still
so much of beauty and of truth to seek?

Why do we spend years acquiring wisdom,
growing in maturity and grace
if, at death, such wisdom as we gain
vanishes into some eternal void?

Physicists now believe that energy
is never lost, but simply changes form;
then why should not the world of the spirit
not destroy but metamorphosize
the essence of our spiritual resources
into some surviving psychic life?

    And at an even deeper level, Lord,
    we wonder why we harbor in our souls
    this yearning for a better, fuller life
    where justice, love, and mercy will prevail.
    You seem to have implanted in our genes
    a universal restless discontent
    with any life that lacks the deep perspective
    which only death and resurrection give.

Therefore, Lord, our key to the enigma
of life and death in this vast universe
clearly is Christ, who links humankind with you;
in him our hopes must ultimately reside.

    Much as ancient man prepared his dead
    to make the journey 'cross the river Styx
    by burying with each sarcophagus
    the jewelry, pots, coins, and clothing needed,
    so, Lord, we ask you to empower
    all of us to stock our minds and spirits
    with the insights, love, compassion, and faith
    we will need to live the future life.

    For Jesus Christ has shown us, Lord,
    that death is not
    a dead end!
                     Amen.

Unholy Spirits

Then let us no more pass judgment on one another, but rather decide never to put a stumbling block or hindrance in the way of a brother. . . . If your brother is being injured by what you eat, you are no longer walking in love. Do not let what you eat cause the ruin of one for whom Christ died. . . . Do not, for the sake of food, destroy the work of God. Everything is indeed clean, but it is wrong for any one to make others fall by what he eats; it is right not to eat meat or drink wine or do anything that makes your brother stumble (Romans 14:13, 15, 20, 21).

Gradually they have been gathering in the cocktail lounge
of a smart suburban banquet facility—
persons from a nearby corporate headquarters
awaiting the beginning of a management dinner.
Suddenly from one end of the polished mahogany bar
comes one of the most sickeningly seductive pleas
it has ever been my misfortune to overhear.

> "Come on, Robert, have a drink on me!
> You've been on the wagon entirely too long.
> It's time you relaxed and lived it up again!"

Bob smiles pleasantly but slowly shakes his head.
"No, thanks. I can't afford to take a chance."

"Don't be stuffy, pal!" persists the enticer.
"It's on me, you know. It'll do you good."

But Bob stands his ground, and I breathe more easily
although I can feel my cheeks glowing hotly
as I bite my lip in anger.

Why am I so angry and upset, Lord?

Because just a few short months earlier
I had seen Bob in the depths of degradation,
unshaven, disheveled, face flushed and voice thick
as he snarled that he was in good shape
and didn't need any God-damned help or sympathy
from me or from anyone else.

The company had granted him a leave of absence
in the hope that he might become rehabilitated,
but neither the efforts of a psychiatrist
nor two "drying out" periods in a private hospital
had brought about any lasting improvement.

Finally, Lord, even Bob came to the grim realization
that he simply couldn't cope with his problem.
Significantly, it was not his minister or church who
finally helped him back to sobriety
and membership once more in the human race;
it was the lay people of Alcoholics Anonymous
whose background of pain, suffering, struggle, and victory
enabled them to empathize with, and minister to, Bob.

How reprehensible, then, was this effort of a "friend"
to undermine Bob's hard-won emotional stability!
Is there any sin more grievous, Lord,
than to thrust temptation in the path of another?
If we are reluctant to be our brother's keeper,
at least we must refrain from being his destroyer.

How sobering it is to contemplate
that in this land full of convivial people
there are more than five million unregenerated Bobs,
while on our nation's crowded highways
fully one-half of the terrible carnage
stems from accidents caused by motorists
who have been moved by "unholy spirits."

Would any other social issue, Lord,
involving 25,000 deaths each year,
as well as injuries and widespread suffering,
fail to stir an outraged response
from concerned church people?

Although drug addiction is receiving much attention,
the use and misuse of alcohol—
simply one type of readily available drug—
seems to occasion little concern,
clothed as it is in an aura of respectability
generated by high-powered advertising
which young people find most appealing.

The basic question confronting thoughtful Christians
is more profound theologically than ethically
or even morally:
Put bluntly, and biblically,
are we to permit our culture and its values
to take precedence
over Christian concern for individuals
and their well-being?
We pose the question in personal terms
because it is the crux of the dilemma.
Liberal main-line churches
are willing to deal with social problems
on a broad bureaucratic basis
through pronouncements,
position papers,
or press releases.

But at the parish level, how many members
fear that taking a stand on the misuse of alcohol
somehow will brand them as being
    prudish,
    puritanical,
    moralistic,
    reactionary,
    old-fashioned,
    and restrictive of personal freedom?

Ah, isn't that the true problem,
interfering with personal freedom!

We Christians deal forthrightly, even sternly,
with the sins of the world
but evasively, if at all,
with the sins in our midst.
Which is to confess, Lord, that we prefer
a parish church that will reinforce, sanction, and condone
    our prejudices,
    our faults,
    our weaknesses,
and keep its hands off our personal lives.

The incongruity of this sort of attitude
is epitomized by the parish committee on ecology
which meets to condemn industry for air pollution
in a room so smoke-filled
that nonsmokers gasp for breath.

Basically our problem is twofold:
First, do we accept the fundamental premise
that to be a Christian imposes on us an obligation
to live responsibly, creatively, compassionately?
    Do we believe that Christians should be identifiable
    not merely by their words and professions of faith
    but also by their consistency in translating those words
    into actions expressing their love and concern
    for their neighbors?
    Are we sensitive to the influence for good or evil
    implicit in our style of life?

Do we realize that in every human community
it is the influential few
who innovate, lead, and set trends
and the masses who observe, follow, and imitate?
Do we understand the social psychology of leadership—
recognized but ignored by many parents—
which purports that any amount of verbal idealism and
    pontificating
is instantly nullified by hypocritical actions
on the part of the leader?

The second aspect of our problem
is infinitely more difficult to sense and to solve
and raises even more related questions:

Are we willing actually to make any necessary changes
in our personal life-styles
so that we no longer will encourage a brother or sister
to falter?
Do we recognize that our personal freedom
must have self-imposed limits
if we are to avoid encroaching on the freedom
of others?
Are we willing to adopt a discipline
and thereby accept restraints for the good of others?
Do we really believe that Christianity
is something to be lived daily
and not merely an intellectual exercise
to be rehearsed on Sundays?
Do we realize that the inside of the cup
should be as clean and stainless as the outside?

In promulgating this course of action, Lord,
let it be understood
that we are not advocating a Pharisaic style of life
such as Christ decried—
a style in which rigid rules and regulations,
prohibitions and taboos
so circumscribe daily living
that they snuff out all sensitivity to the human aspects
which should govern our conduct.

On the contrary, we are seeking to emphasize
that the responsible Christian life is a *relational* life
in which every choice, every decision, every action
should be viewed as it relates to others.

Does a contemplated move
    help or hinder,
    strengthen or weaken,
    elevate or denigrate,
    free or enslave,
    cheer or sadden
a spouse, a child, a friend, a neighbor, a community?
Living as we do in a complex, fast-moving,
stress-filled world,
we will find it difficult, yet our bounden duty,
to think through the ultimate effect on others
of what we plan to do and then
test it against Christ's teachings and example.

Christianity should not be limited, Lord,
    to helping the oppressed,
    rescuing the downtrodden,
    feeding the hungry,
    clothing the naked.
Instead, we should practice *preventative* Christianity
and thereby seek to ally ourselves
with the moral and ethical forces
at work in our society.

    Too much of our time, energy, and effort is spent
    in binding up wounds
    and not enough in striving to avoid
    inflicting wounds!

So grant us the wisdom, the patience, and the strength
through your Holy Spirit, Lord,
to help render harmless and ineffective
all unholy spirits.

Amen.

On Breaking the Vicious Cycle

"But I say to you, Do not resist one who is evil. But if any one strikes you on the right cheek, turn to him the other also; and if any one would sue you and take your coat, let him have your cloak as well; and if any one forces you to go one mile, go with him two miles" (Matthew 5:39-41).

How difficult it is, Lord,
to follow your precepts
in this modern world of ours
where evil persons acquire great power
by throwing their weight around
without regard for human rights,
human dignity,
or human sensibilities.

You tell us, Lord, how we should react
to belligerent actions we encounter—
> someone striking my right cheek,
> or taking my coat,

or forcing me to go one mile
    (presumably against my will
    and at a time
    and in a direction
    I do not choose to go!).
And you admonish me, Lord,
to turn the other cheek,
to give my adversary my cloak as well,
to go yet another mile—
    all these against my natural inclination
    to strike back,
    to cling to my possessions,
    to resist being shoved around.

Somehow, Lord, with your help and guidance
I sometimes find the strength
to meet these challenges
when they involve physical actions
such as you describe
    (although I have become quite expert
    at turning my back
    and avoiding someone's troubled gaze
    before he or she can disturb my comfort!).

But great is my pain and anguish, Lord,
when, instead of facing violence,
I find myself confronted by another
    seeking to win some point,
    or beat me down
    or tear me apart
through the cunning use of ridicule
or taunting threats
or cruel caustic comment.

It is mental and emotional hurts
such as these induce
which most abrade my ego,
shrivel my soul,
and fill me with bitterness.

That is when retaliation
by equally angry rejoinder
seems natural and deserved,
whereas walking a second verbal mile
in tight-lipped silence
confronts me with the yawning pitfalls
of injured pride and self-pity.

And then I hear the shrink
warn of subservience and surrender
and urge assertiveness and retaliation:
    "Don't take it lying down;
    Don't warp your personality;
    Don't risk inducing neuroses
    by sublimating others' aggressiveness
    to fancied religious piety;
    instead, let it all hang out!
    Lash back and, for a change,
    put the bastards on the defensive!
    An eye for an eye, a tooth for a tooth,
    is the only language most persons comprehend;
    use it, and preserve your mental health."

There, Lord, is the troubling tension
between what is and what should be;
between the unreality of the world's reality
into which you have plunged us
and the eternal reality
of what you proclaim
in thought, word, and deed.

Yet from the living pages of the past
breathes testimony from the faithful few—
the sighs of martyrs, valiant to the end,
whispers from saints enshrined in memory—
while hovering over, under, and around
like some far-off yet near celestial force
is that majestic cloud of witnesses,
    the remnant who steadfastly kept the faith
    and risked their all
    for you.

But, Lord, how well you understand our pain,
for you were ridiculed and vilified,
pursued by angry, fearful, cunning men
until we hear you crying from the cross:
"Father, forgive . . . they know not what they do."

Forgive *us*, Father; we know not what *we* do
to the hearts, minds, and souls
    of those of other faiths,
    other races,
    other cultures
by claiming that we alone possess the truth
then proving that we don't
    by imposing on others the very pressures
    and prejudices
    and judgments
we resent when applied to us.

What is the answer, Lord?
How can we melt away our hardness of heart,
our preoccupation with self,
our insensitivity to others?
How can we overcome
this Stone Age mentality
which is our inheritance
from a million years of savagery?

But you gave us the answer, didn't you?
An answer so simple
    we resist it,
an answer so difficult to apply
    we avoid it,
an answer so close at hand
    we search instead for more remote solutions.

    It is "love your enemies
    and pray for those who persecute you. . . .
    For if you love those who love you,
    what reward have you?"

Yes, Lord, a climate of love, trust, and goodwill
can set the stage for new beginnings
by enabling us to overcome
our perverse urge to retaliate!
The soft answer *can* turn away wrath;
the warm smile *can* melt hostility;
openness to the spirit *can* allay suspicion
if we but sublimate our pride to you.

So help us to be obedient, Lord,
and we may even find
we can turn the other cheek
without losing face!

Amen.

*The Scripture quoted in the text of this prayer
is found in Matthew 5:44, 46.*

Last Word

"Yet your people say: 'The way of the Lord is not just'; when it is their own way that is not just. When the righteous turns from his righteousness, and commits iniquity, he shall die for it. And when the wicked turns from his wickedness and does what is lawful and right, he shall live by it. Yet you say, 'The way of the Lord is not just.' O house of Israel, I will judge each of you according to his ways" (Ezekiel 33:17-20).

For an all-powerful deity, Lord,
you really have messed things up, haven't you?

We gaze about us and see the turmoil in the world
with the third-world nations
trying to claw their way upward,
the overprivileged callously clinging to their wealth,
armaments proliferating
as "merchants of death" promote their wares,
concerned women lobbying against male domination,
politicians conniving with special interests,
labor leaders feuding with businessmen and industrialists,

environmentalists zealously assailing polluters,
dictators ruthlessly suppressing human rights,
criminals terrorizing inner-city ghettos,
teenage thugs assaulting teachers and guards,
and everywhere disillusionment, desperation, and despair
as the frustrated seek a scapegoat
responsible for the mess.

    How can we possibly forgive you, Lord,
    for thrusting us into the midst
    of this kind of world?
    For perpetrating on us
    a cruel hoax?
    For exposing us to the meaninglessness,
    the senselessness,
    the idiocy
    of an existence where truth does not prevail,
    where ends seldom justify the means,
    where beauty is sacrificed for ugly ambition,
    and where evil has an unpleasant way of triumphing
    over righteousness?

How much better, Lord, *we* would have done the job
if only you had entrusted the task of creation to us!
Then humanity would have possessed a nobility of character
replete with spiritual vitality, integrity, and honor;
compassion would have governed our human relations
with justice and mercy prevailing for all;
humankind's senseless struggle to dominate and enslave
      others
would have been replaced by sharing, serving, and love;
and all of . . .

    But what in the name of God are we saying?
    What hideous heresy are we voicing?
    How distorted can our rationalizing become?

For you *did* create an idyllic world, Lord,
with an amazing variety and ecological balance
    of flora and fauna,
    birds and insects,
    animals and fishes,
and, as well, an ingenious support system
    of sun and rain,
    moon and tides,
    wind and clouds,
    heat and cold,
    fire and flood.

Then, creating persons in your own image,
you placed them in charge of this wonderful world,
giving them dominion over land and sea
and all the teeming life above and below.

    Yet, in spite of receiving your managerial appointment
    to administer this Garden of Eden,
    Adam (aided and abetted by Eve)
    chose to disobey you and violate your trust,
    his reason and conscience blinded by the arrogant
        assumption
    that equality with God is a thing to be grasped.

And so today, Lord, we look back
almost indulgently
to the allegorical account of Adam's fall from grace
and regard "sin" as little more
than a quaint form of disobedience
as ancient as the world, as historic as the Old Testament,
but of precious little relevance to
our post-Christian era.

Then how cleverly and blithely we rationalize
that with "sin" thus an inherited, but minor,
aspect of our natures,
we really aren't responsible, or accountable,
for whatever evil we may do;
nor are we under obligation to repent,
to make restitution,
nor even to reform our self-centered, perverse selves.

> For after all, Lord, didn't your Son give us assurance
> that you are a merciful and forgiving God?
> (Although *even your* patience with us
> must be getting sorely strained!)

So join the fellowship of fools, you modern Adams and Eves,
and, adopting the advice of Luther,
"sin on bravely,"
> for sin is a word we have stricken from our vocabulary,
> and morality is a state of mind we define
> according to gut reaction and transient need.

In its place we have plucked from your tree of knowledge,
        Lord,
a new and wonderful fruit called "science"
which harbors within its pithy core
all the seeds for human betterment or destruction.
Although Jesus reminded us that
        "A disciple is not above his teacher,
        nor a servant above his master;
        it is enough for the disciple to be like his teacher,
        and the servant like his master,"
we find our technological knowledge and power so heady,
        Lord,
that we feel positively godlike in our modern Garden of Eden.
                                                        1
And having shed our former concern for personal morality
and the many sins it encompassed against friend or
        neighbor—
        jealousy, anger, and envy,
        sexual misbehavior and unfaithfulness,
        dishonesty of thought and deed,
        avarice, greed, and slander—
we now find ourselves confronted with new and disturbing
social sins—
sins so frightening in their awesome dimensions
they are capable of inflicting suffering and destruction
not merely on persons we encounter
during life's pilgrimage
but also upon innocent millions
we neither see, know, nor wish to harm.

        What, then, are these sins against society
        which now confront us?
        And in what way could we possibly be involved?
        Are we perhaps guilty of tacit approval through
        indifference?
        Through unwillingness to become involved
        in opposing the forces of evil?

Whatever the explanation, Lord, we all share in the guilt
of littering and polluting and defiling
by adding to the effluent of an affluent society
and in the process desecrating
the Eden-like environment you bestowed upon us.

And if this were not sin enough,
we greedily consume a disproportionate share
of the earth's bounty,
closing our eyes, our ears, our hearts, and our consciences
to widespread starvation, infant mortality, and short life span
among those less fortunate.

And then, as if our existence on this planet
were not sufficiently precarious,
we strive to devise
new forms of atomic, bacterial, and laser warfare;
we callously condone, or participate in,
many types of persecution
(of which the most heinous was the Holocaust),
all the while contemplating
even more subtle and manipulative sins:
electronic surveillance of entire populations,
thought control and enslavement through drugs,
genetic engineering with all its potential
for creating fiendish personalities
or robotlike compliance.

> Yet we dare to accuse *you*, Lord,
> of responsibility for this mess!
> We moan that you have deserted us when, in truth,
> we have turned our backs on you!

Is there hope for us?
Not merely for our salvation, Lord,
but also for the future of humanity?
Can we become obedient and reverse our egocentric course
before we self-destruct?

Dare we hope, Lord, that you will use us
to help change the values, the goals, the climate
of this so-called civilization?
To work out your purpose for us and the human race?
To feed the hungry, to give drink to the thirsty,
To welcome the stranger, to clothe the naked,
To visit the sick and the imprisoned?
Can we really become, in Paul's challenging words,
"mature in Christ"?

> Our hope, Lord, lies in your Son's assurance that
> "with God, all things are possible!"
> With God. With God! *That* is the clue!

For you are the creator, the dramatist,
the producer, the director
of this unfolding drama of life
you have destined us to live out.
All the world's your stage,
and we are the unpredictable actors and actresses.
When the original cast
failed to follow your direction,
you sent to earth an incredible impressario
to show us, by word and by example,
how humankind might achieve greatness.
But for the past two thousand years, Lord,
we have muffed our lines,
quarreled in the wings,
ignored the director,
and used the thespian skills and freedom you have given us,
not to turn in a virtuoso performance
that would help bring about your kingdom,
but instead to glorify our egos
by upstaging our fellow actors,
by playing to the gallery,
and by reversing the billing
so that the performers appear to be greater
than the playwright.

How long will you sadly watch us, Lord,
make a travesty of your beautiful drama?
How long will you forgive our frailties,
pardon our prima donna pretensions,
tolerate our tampering with your scenario?
How long before you ring down the curtain
and turn out the house lights?

Will we realize in time
that you are both playwright and critic,
that yours is the last and final word?

Amen.

*The Scripture quoted in the text of this prayer
is from Matthew 10:24-25.*